PRAISE FOR *HARBIN*

"This is a powerful word for our times, and crucial for those who would be a part of the next great move of God. It is a word that does need to be read by every Christian, and I have no doubt will be studied by serious disciples of the King of kings."

—Rick Joyner, founder and executive director of MorningStar Ministries; author of more than fifty books, including *The Vision*

"This book is truly a beacon of hope for this generation. Just as a lighthouse, this will guide you and impart hope and faith into your life. You will be inspired to believe! Robin has written a book that truly reflects his heart and life. He has personally impacted my life and I have no doubt you will feel that same hope-filled power explode in your life!"

—Pastor James Levesque, Engaging Heaven Church, 66 Union Street, New London, Connecticut

"Wagonloads of hope are coming your way! Reading this book has brought a greater bounce of joy and hope into my life, and I know it will do the same thing for you. Discover the you God has made you to be—a Harbinger of Hope to the world! Every chapter is loaded with insights. Read it as God's message to you and it will change your life. And be sure to get a copy for a friend, your friend will thank you for it!"

—Brian Simmons, The Passion Translation Project

"Thanks, Robin McMillan, for this tsunami of hope. It is difficult to believe that so much truth is packed into a tome of less than 225 pages! I have practiced something with this book that I have never chosen to do until now: I have moved through it from front to finish and then turned around and went from back to beginning. It has been a personal thrust of fresh hope for me. It is power driven, life giving, hope stirring, and prophetically empowered. Thanks, Robin, for the lift!"

—Jack Taylor, president, Dimensions Ministries, Melbourne, Florida

"There is no greater message needed today than the message of hope. The Bible makes it clear to us that we have been redeemed into a living hope, yet it seems to be a truth that we struggle to believe in and fail to lean on. Hope is a foundational issue in our lives from which so many things flow. Robin McMillan in *Harbinger of Hope* does a brilliant job of not only laying a clear foundation of truth for your life but will speak hope to your souls and awaken your hearts. It is timely, powerful, profound, and much needed for the body of Christ."

—Banning Liebscher, Jesus Culture founder and pastor

"I love Robin McMillan's new book. This is a time when hope seems to be rare. Politics disappoint. Relationships disappoint, and frankly the church seems to lack a true revelation of our hope in Jesus. I love that Joseph's wagons of guaranteed proof are on their way to establish our hope. The gospel of Jesus can empower us constantly and fill the hope tank, deploying us into a hope-starved world. Read this encouraging book and begin hoping!"

—Steve Witt, Bethel, Cleveland

"Robin opens up his heart and unique understandings to the reader. The scriptural instruction and his testimonies of revelatory experiences is a potent combination that will challenge and edify the believer. Do you want your hope strengthened? Read this book. I did, and mine was."

—David Harwood, pastor, Restoration Fellowship, Glen Cove, New York; author of *God's True Love* and *For the Sake of the Fathers*

"Have you ever found yourself feeling hopeless? Feeling that *all* hope is gone? In *Harbinger of Hope*, Robin McMillan weaves together a practical approach to a hope-filled life. He will: Open your ears—to hear hope. Open your eyes—to see hope. Open your heart—to receive hope. It is a book of revelation, visitation, impartation, and activation. Read it and let it read you."

—Leif Hetland, author, *Giant Slayers*

"I was in Houston getting ready to preach when the Lord brought Robin's book to mind. I tried to skim through it but found myself captivated by Robin's prophetic gift and powerful revelations. I was soon poring over every page—highlighting entire paragraphs. I am a voracious reader and can tell you that this does not happen often. Robin's book is a five-course meal. Don't know when I've read so many unique and compelling insights and powerful prophetic testimonies in such an easy to read, enjoyable manuscript. This is the perfect book to set you up for the move of God that is coming!"

—Dr. Lance Wallnau, Lance Learning Group, Lance@Lancelearning.com

"Robin McMillian inspires us to examine our calling in God's kingdom . . . and to use our unique giftedness to proclaim *hope* for our world."

—Rick Eldridge, film producer, *The Ultimate Gift, Bobby Jones: Stroke of Genius, Four Blood Moons*

"In the pages of *Harbinger of Hope*, Robin McMillan has invited us to ascend above the toxic atmosphere of today's culture and breathe the fresh air of hope! Today, when many can easily find a problem in any solution, Robin provides a much needed perspective that is both prophetic and practical. Drawing from his personal encounters with God and from the timeless biblical text, he lights the way forward. I have known this man for almost thirty years and can assure you that he epitomizes what it means to be a true Harbinger of Hope."

—Dr. Randall Worley, author of *Brush Strokes of Grace* and *Wandering & Wondering*

HARBINGER

of

HOPE

HARBINGER
of
HOPE

A STARTLING REVELATION OF GOD'S
GREAT PROVISION FOR YOU

ROBIN
McMILLAN

EMANATE
BOOKS

Published in Nashville, Tennessee, by Emanate Books, an imprint of Thomas Nelson. Nelson Books and Thomas Nelson are registered trademarks of HarperCollins Christian Publishing, Inc.

Thomas Nelson titles may be purchased in bulk for educational, business, fund-raising, or sales promotional use. For information, please e-mail SpecialMarkets@ThomasNelson.com.

Unless otherwise noted, Scripture quotations are taken from the New King James Version®. © 1982 by Thomas Nelson. Used by permission. All rights reserved.

Scripture quotations marked THE MESSAGE are from *The Message*. Copyright © by Eugene H. Peterson 1993, 1994, 1995, 1996, 2000, 2001, 2002. Used by permission of NavPress. All rights reserved. Represented by Tyndale House Publishers, Inc.

Scripture quotations marked NASB are from New American Standard Bible®. Copyright © 1960, 1962, 1963, 1968, 1971, 1972, 1973, 1975, 1977, 1995 by The Lockman Foundation. Used by permission. (www.Lockman.org)

Scripture quotations marked TLB are from The Living Bible. Copyright © 1971. Used by permission of Tyndale House Publishers, Inc., Carol Stream, Illinois 60188. All rights reserved.

Scripture quotations marked VUL are from The Latin Vulgate. Public domain.

Scripture quotations marked LXX are from the Brenton translation of the Septuagint LXX. Public domain.

Scripture quotations marked TPT are taken from The Passion Translation®. Copyright © 2017 by BroadStreet Publishing® Group, LLC. Used by permission. All rights reserved. thePassionTranslation.com.

Scripture quotations marked WET are from *The New Testament: An Expanded Translation* by Kenneth S. Wuest, © Wm. B. Eerdmans Publishing Co. 1961. All rights reserved.

Scripture quotations marked AMP are from the Amplified˙ Bible, copyright © 1954, 1958, 1962, 1964, 1965, 1987 by The Lockman Foundation. Used by permission. (www.Lockman.org)

Scripture quotations marked KJV are from the King James Version, public domain.

Emphasis in Scripture verses has been added by the author.

ISBN 978-0-7852-2080-0 (eBook)
ISBN 978-0-7852-2079-4 (TP)

Library of Congress Control Number: 2018943312

Printed in the United States of America

18 19 20 21 22 LSC 10 9 8 7 6 5 4 3 2 1

I dedicate *Harbinger of Hope* to my wife, Donna.
She has been God's best gift to me.

—Robin McMillan

Contents

Contents

FOREWORD

I love how Robin McMillan thinks. He has a unique ability to see things in Scripture that others miss. His perspective is always original, redemptive, and filled with hope, as this book accurately displays. *Harbinger of Hope* is aptly named. It is filled with practical, yet profound, insights into God's intentions for our lifetime. I don't think this book could be released in a timelier season than right now. Countless numbers of believers will no doubt be launched into divine encounters that change how we impact the world. Read and learn. Study and be transformed.

Bill Johnson
Bethel Church, Redding, California
Author of *When Heaven Invades Earth*
and *God Is Good*

Part One

HARBINGER OF HOPE

One

My Prophetic Encounter

I lay in bed early one morning in a hotel room feeling oppressed and exhausted even after a good night's sleep. It was a familiar kind of spiritual challenge I sometimes encounter just before speaking in a conference. I knew I must go on the offensive. So, alone in my room I began to exercise faith and enforce my authority. As an act of warfare I proclaimed a personalized version of Psalm 91 from memory:

> He who dwells in the secret place of the Most High shall abide under the shadow of the Almighty, whose power no evil foe can withstand. I will say of the LORD, "He is my refuge, He is my fortress; my God, on Him will I lean and rely, and in Him I will confidently trust." Surely then He shall deliver me from the snare of the fowler and from the perilous pestilence. He shall cover me with His feathers, and under His wings I shall take refuge; His truth shall be my shield and buckler.

God will release the power of His Word as we believe it and proclaim it. As I spoke these verses, God's enabling power strengthened my soul. I determined that if quoting Psalm 91 once was good, twice would be even better. So with renewed strength and even more conviction, I proclaimed His truth aloud once more. I set my defeated enemy on the run as I again said, "He who dwells in the secret place of the Most High shall abide under the shadow of the Almighty. . . ."

As I finished quoting these verses a second time, I saw an opening in the ceiling that wasn't there before. I just knew that I was supposed to jump up into it. So I did. As I was passing through, I could hear demons screaming, "Stop. You can't come through here!" But I laughed at them because they couldn't stop me. Suddenly I found myself in what seemed to be a heavenly realm. It was unlike anything I had ever seen or experienced before, and I knew I was about to encounter the Lord in a remarkable and supernatural way.

At first I didn't understand why it wasn't bright. After all, this was a heavenly place. Then I noticed a huge wing above me and realized I was under its shadow. I was further confused because I assumed the wing must be an angel's and should be brilliantly white, but it was dark brown. Then I understood. *Had I not just boldly proclaimed that I would dwell in the secret place of the Most High and abide under the shadow of the Almighty? Had I not declared that He would deliver me from the snare of the fowler—you know, the bird catcher? That's quite a specific promise for a man named Robin!* Had I not emphatically proclaimed, *He shall cover me with His feathers, and under His wings I shall take refuge?* I was not under a large angel's wing but had found refuge under the massive wing of the Great Eagle, the One whom I had just boldly proclaimed.

The wing was amazing. Grapefruit-size precious stones emanated from the underside. Gold and silver particles and other precious metals emanated from the wing as well. They were not just attached, but actually came out of it. I had never seen anything like that before. The very essence of the Eagle was made of precious resources of incalculable worth.

Five Supernatural Wagons of Blessing

Then my attention was drawn to five wagons. Each wagon was crammed to overflowing with divine substance. I did not see the physical items with my natural eyes, but I knew instinctively that each wagon carried an abundance of spiritual blessing that is available to God's people. Doesn't God's Word promise us that He has "blessed us with every spiritual blessing in the heavenly places in Christ" (Eph. 1:3)? I could hardly contain myself as I considered what I saw.

The first wagon contained deliverance from deserved consequences.
The second wagon contained deliverance from criticism and the critical spirit.
The third wagon carried abundant hope.
The fourth wagon held unlimited provision.
And the fifth wagon had a new vision for the United States.

The Story of Joseph

I instinctively knew—with a knowledge that transcends seeing and learning in the normal way—that I would discover the deeper significance of my startling encounter in the story of Joseph and the restoration of his family. Joseph's story is one of great hope. Joseph was Jacob's favorite son. That alone was enough to make Joseph's brothers jealous. But their jealousy turned to hatred when Joseph described several prophetic dreams that indicated they would all bow down to him and serve him one day. Joseph's attitude and the substance of those dreams infuriated his brothers.

When Joseph was seventeen years old, Jacob sent him to check on his brothers who had gone to graze their father's flocks. When they saw him coming from a distance, they conspired to kill him. At Reuben's insistence, they spared Joseph's life but threw him into a pit. Later they sold him to traveling Ishmaelite merchants who sold him to Potiphar, the captain of the guards of Pharaoh, king of Egypt. Joseph's brothers covered his colorful outer garment in blood and returned it to their father. With the blood-soaked coat in his hands, Jacob concluded his favorite son had been devoured by wild animals. Believing that lie devastated Jacob for twenty-two years.

As an Egyptian slave Joseph excelled in all he did. Potiphar admired him and promoted him to oversee his entire household and eventually govern all he had. But alas, his favor would not go unchallenged.

Potiphar's wife repeatedly propositioned Joseph. When he rebuffed her she falsely accused him of making sexual advances. Potiphar imprisoned him in the jail reserved specifically for the king's prisoners. Yet even in prison God favored the young Hebrew. The keeper of the prison granted him authority over all the other prisoners. Joseph met the royal baker and butler, both imprisoned by Pharaoh for various offenses.

One night both of Pharaoh's former stewards had dreams they did not understand. The next morning after they told Joseph their dreams, he interpreted them with pinpoint accuracy. Three days later, as Joseph had predicted, Pharaoh executed the baker for treason but restored the butler to his original place of service. Time passed and then Pharaoh himself had two dreams that his magicians and wise men could not interpret.

The butler then remembered Joseph and told Pharaoh about him. Troubled by his dreams, Pharaoh quickly summoned Joseph from the dungeon to see if he could interpret them. Joseph would not disappoint him.

Joseph appeared before Pharaoh and explained the meaning of the dreams. He discerned that Egypt would have seven years of great bounty followed by seven years of famine so severe it would deplete the abundant harvest of the first seven years. He also provided the king with wisdom for preserving life through the years of famine. Pharaoh was to store the vast amount of produce during the fat years to sustain his nation during the lean ones, and he should appoint a wise and discerning man to assure the success of that plan.

Joseph so impressed Pharaoh that he set him in authority over all the land of Egypt. Only Pharaoh had greater authority in the nation. Just as the dreams had predicted, there were seven years of abundant harvest that turned to famine in the eighth year. Joseph's plan to store bounty from the first seven prosperous years would preserve many lives during the seven lean years. The great famine decimated Egypt's agriculture and that of the surrounding nations. Starvation threatened millions of people, extending all the way to the door of Jacob's household. When Jacob learned that there was grain in Egypt, in utter desperation the patriarch ordered his sons to go to Egypt for food. Unbeknownst to them Joseph controlled the great storehouses of Egypt.

A LONG TWENTY-TWO YEARS

When Joseph was a naïve and inexperienced man of seventeen, his own brothers' callous hearts betrayed him, and he became a slave in Egypt. But by the age of thirty, by God's providence, he became the second most powerful man in the kingdom. Then, nine years later, in the second year of the famine, his brothers arrived in Egypt seeking food for survival. Twenty-two long, turbulent years after their terrible betrayal, the brothers stood as beggars before Joseph. They did not recognize him, but he immediately knew who they were. God alone understood what Joseph felt about his brothers as they stood there. Before helping them he put them through a grueling process. But this we do know: God did such a redemptive work in Joseph's heart that he determined to save the lives of his brothers and father.

When Joseph finally revealed his true identity to his eleven brothers, he did so with many tears and much brokenness. He first simply wanted to know if his father was still alive. Then he implored his brothers to come close to him, to neither be grieved nor angry with themselves for what they had done. He explained that it was God who had sent him before them to preserve their lives during the famine. He wanted them to go back home and tell Jacob what had become of Joseph and to bring Jacob and his household to the nearby town of Goshen, where Joseph could care for them during the next five years of famine.

When the news reached Pharaoh, he was pleased, and he supported Joseph's decision to tell his brothers to return home and bring their father and their families back to Egypt. He also told Joseph to let his brothers know that in addition to provisions for the journey he wanted them to take wagons with them for their father, their wives, and children, and then return.

THE SIGNIFICANCE OF THE WAGONS: JACOB REVIVES

The great historic *revival* of the house of Jacob began when Joseph gave his brothers wagons, as Pharaoh had commanded, and sent them to return safely with Jacob and his family. The wagons would prove to be of special significance to Jacob. They became the vehicles that restored Jacob and his family to Joseph and saved their entire lineage. When Jacob's sons finally returned to the land of Canaan and told him that Joseph was still alive and governor over all the land of Egypt, "Jacob's heart fainted, for he believed them not. And they told him all the words of Joseph, which he had said unto them: and *when he saw the wagons* which Joseph had sent to carry him, the spirit of Jacob their father revived: And *Israel* said, It is enough; Joseph my son is yet alive: I will go and see him before I die" (Gen. 45:26–28 KJV).

The news that Joseph was alive had so shocked his father that *Jacob's heart stood still* in unbelief. His disappointment and despair had deep, decades-long roots. But then a most remarkable transformation occurred. As the brothers told Jacob what Joseph had said about the last twenty-two years of his life, and then as he saw the wagons, the extent of God's great goodness and His abundant provision caused hope to spring up in Jacob's heart. But then the Bible reveals something else even more remarkable: "And then Israel said . . ." Jacob became Israel!

There is also a significant prophetic promise for our nation, and for the church in particular, contained in this story. Jacob is much like many in the American church, living in unbelief, languishing in a spiritual famine, wondering if they will survive this wilderness. Can you believe that God has an answer for us even in the face of all our trouble, all the negativity and financial difficulty, all the harsh and troubling news that surrounds us? He does. He is not through showing Himself strong on our behalf. Nothing catches God by surprise and He is never left without a solution. The Scripture assures our ultimate victory in every situation: "Now thanks be to God who always leads us in triumph in Christ, and through us diffuses the fragrance of His knowledge in every place" (2 Cor. 2:14).

Hearing Joseph's words and seeing Joseph's wagons transformed Jacob in a most remarkable way: "The spirit of Jacob their father revived" (Gen. 45:27), and he became known as Israel (v. 28), the new name the Lord gave him when he prevailed at the ford of Jabbok years earlier. That is the first time the word *revive* is used in the Bible. Just as seeing the wagons Joseph sent sparked revival and restoration in the house of Jacob, the reality of the substance in the five wagons in my encounter can revive everyone who accesses them. Just as God sent Joseph ahead of them twenty-two years before, He sent Jesus before us and has provided everything we need. Believing the message of His provision in those five wagons has the potential to revive you and your family and to release revival to our nation. God is restoring hope!

That early morning as I struggled in my hotel room, my experience became a harbinger. A harbinger is a forerunner, a person or thing that announces the approach of something significant. Being caught up under the wing of the Great Eagle and discovering the five wagons of God's unique provision for our generation was a harbinger indeed—a harbinger of hope!

Two

THE FIVE WAGONS

Joseph is an important type of the Lord Jesus, one of the clearest in all the Old Testament. Bible commentators have identified more than sixty similarities the two share. For instance, the disciples thought Jesus was dead; He was not only alive but Lord of all. For years Jacob thought Joseph was dead, but he was alive and, except for Pharaoh, lord of all Egypt. Both Jesus and Joseph were hated by their brethren, were sorely tempted yet prevailed, involuntarily taken to Egypt, stripped of their robes, sold for the price of a slave, falsely accused, wrongly caused to suffer, exalted after suffering, gracious to forgive those who wronged them, rescuers of their people, loved by and obedient to their fathers, and were both faithful servants. Jesus released the reviving power of the Holy Spirit to the world that continues to this day, while Joseph revived the household of Jacob when he sent the wagons to his father. Joseph not only saved their lives but preserved the lineage of the Messiah.

Even though Joseph was betrayed by his brothers and suffered great difficulties because of their jealousy, he loved his family. At least six different times in Genesis 45 he reassured them of his love and

11

commitment to restore them and provide a new and better life for them: "Please come near to me" (v. 4); "God has made me lord of all Egypt; come down to me, do not tarry" (v. 9); "You shall be near to me, you and your children, your children's children" (v. 10); "There I will provide for you" (v. 11); "You shall hurry and bring my father down here" (v. 13); "Moreover he kissed all his brothers and wept over them" (v. 15). Then in chapter 47 it says, "Then Joseph provided his father, his brothers, and all his father's household with bread" (Gen. 47:12).

Joseph demonstrated an extraordinarily redemptive heart toward his brothers. Jesus is the "greater Joseph." As forgiving as the compassionate words of Joseph are, they are but a shallow picture of the compassion Jesus feels toward each of us. Joseph lived for his brothers and his father. Jesus died for His enemies. Can you hear the Master's pleas in Joseph's simple words? Just as Jacob revived when he heard the words of Joseph, saw the camels bearing abundant provision, and the great wagons sent to take them to the safety of Egypt, we, too, will revive as we believe the good news of Jesus and see the amazing resources of heaven He has provided for us. This abundant provision is what God revealed to me in the five wagons of my encounter.

WAGON ONE: DELIVERANCE FROM DESERVED CONSEQUENCES

The first wagon I saw was filled with provision for *deliverance from deserved consequences.* Jesus loves people so much that He wants to set them free from the deserved effects of their bad choices and decisions, even their deliberate ones. The prophet Isaiah accurately portrayed the heart of Jesus many years before His earthly pilgrimage when he proclaimed, "He shall see of the travail of his soul, and shall be satisfied: by his knowledge shall my righteous servant justify many; for he shall bear their iniquities" (Isa. 53:11 KJV).

Perhaps you did the wrong thing, you made the wrong choice—yes, you sinned—but Jesus wants to set you free from what you deserve and deliver you from the consequences of your actions. He paid an exorbitant price to redeem us. He will not stop until we have fully received all He has for us.

Wagon Two: Deliverance from Criticism and the Critical Spirit

The second wagon in my vision contained provision for *deliverance from criticism and the critical spirit*. We need to be delivered from both to fulfill our purpose in life. Spoken words have power, and criticism has damaged many people. Being critical of others is equally destructive to those who criticize. Jesus warned that we would be condemned to the same degree that we continue to condemn others. Jesus can deliver wounded people from both the effects of other people's criticisms and from being critical themselves.

Wagon Three: Abundant Hope

The third wagon overflowed with *abundant hope*. Hope is vital, having the capacity to produce robust faith, for "faith is the substance of things hoped for, the evidence of things not seen" (Heb. 11:1). The apostle Paul said that hope anchors our souls, protects our minds, and initiates a life of faith.

Hopelessness is a consequence, not a cause. It is a delusion, the fruit of believing lies. Jesus said we would know the truth and the truth would set us free (John 8:32). One who knows who Jesus is and believes the truth is filled with a hope that cannot be extinguished. The book of Proverbs tells us that "hope deferred makes the heart sick" (Prov. 13:12). Many people do not maintain their hope until the promised breakthrough comes. But no one, no situation, no circumstance has the right or power to defer your hope but you.

WAGON FOUR: UNLIMITED PROVISION

The fourth wagon I saw was laden with *unlimited provision*. God has provided everything we need and deposited it in heaven for us. Jesus taught us to pray, "Your kingdom come. Your will be done on earth as it is in heaven" (Matt. 6:10), meaning that God intends for us to use our faith to access and release on earth what heaven contains for the benefit of all. There are no poor people in heaven, no sick and no depressed. During Jesus' earthly ministry He lived from that realm not only to help the people of His day but to encourage us and model for us a lifestyle we also can have today. We must simply learn how to access the bounty of heaven that is available by faith now, for "the kingdom of heaven is at hand" (Matt. 10:7).

WAGON FIVE: A NEW VISION
FOR THE UNITED STATES

The fifth wagon I witnessed was filled with the blessing of *a new vision for the United States*. When Joseph brought his family to live in

Egypt, Pharaoh provided the best land for their home. He gave them a land called Goshen, which means "drawing near."[1] The name offers a clue as to what will bring transformation to our own land. Scripture says, "Draw near to God and He will draw near to you" (James 4:8). If believers in our nation draw near to God, He will draw near to us and change our nation. I believe that will happen in the United States of America. We are on the verge of another spiritual great awakening that will reshape our culture.

The divine treasures laden in these five wagons seem too good to be true. Or are they?

Part Two

WAGON ONE: DELIVERANCE FROM DESERVED CONSEQUENCES

Three

EXPERIENCING GOD'S DELIVERANCE AND RESTORATION

Until the good news of the grace of God seems too good to be true, we have not yet seen it in all its fullness. The provision in the first wagon—the blessing of "deliverance from deserved consequences"— truly seemed too good to be true. Will God deliver us from what we deserve? Yes. God forgives and restores. If He didn't, no one would be redeemed and no one would make it to heaven.

The Bible is clear: "All have sinned and fall short of the glory of God" (Rom. 3:23), and "the soul who sins shall die" (Ezek. 18:20). Jesus said, "I will show you whom you should fear: Fear Him who, after He has killed, has power to cast into hell; yes, I say to you, fear Him!" (Luke 12:5). These sobering words testify that we all need deliverance from what we deserve. The death, burial, and resurrection of Christ Jesus provided the only way of deliverance from ultimate *deserved consequences*.

True repentance is the key to experiencing this forgiveness. We must turn not only *from* whatever deserves His condemnation but also *toward* God and renew our minds completely. Without complete repentance we will never fully experience both the depth of God's mercy and the breadth of His redemption.

THE APOSTLE PETER

Jesus delivered Simon Peter from deserved consequences more than once. During Jesus' betrayal in the Garden of Gethsemane, Peter attacked Malchus, the chief officer of the high priest. "One of them struck the servant of the high priest and cut off his right ear. But Jesus answered and said, 'Permit even this.' And He touched his ear and healed him" (Luke 22:50–51). By that criminal act alone Peter deserved crucifixion. But Jesus touched Malchus's ear and healed him.

The word *touched* means "to attach to" and the word *healed* means to "make whole." Jesus may have simply picked up Malchus's ear and reattached it to his head. However Jesus did it, He healed the man, destroyed the evidence of Peter's crime, and saved him from a premature crucifixion for the attempted murder of the servant of the high priest. God can deliver us from deserved consequences and may even destroy the evidence of our failure.

THE APOSTLE PAUL: GRACE ENLARGED

Acts 7 introduces Saul of Tarsus as he approved the death of Stephen, the first Christian martyr. Stephen, an original deacon, was full of the Holy Spirit and faith. He did great signs and wonders and incurred the wrath of the Synagogue of the Freedmen (Acts 6:9). They could neither refute his wisdom nor withstand the Spirit by which he spoke, so they framed him, accused him of blasphemy, and brought him before the Jewish high council.

Stephen defended himself before the high priest. He outlined God's plan through a discourse of the history of His dealings with Israel, beginning with Abraham and ending with the promise of the Messiah. Stephen rebuked them for having rejected the prophets of old and for killing the Messiah Himself. The council ground their teeth in anger as they cast him out and stoned him to death. Saul of Tarsus stood by, consenting to Stephen's death. Afterward, Saul began a focused attack on the believers in Jerusalem:

> Now Saul was consenting to his death. At that time a great persecution arose against the church which was at Jerusalem; and they were all scattered throughout the regions of Judea and Samaria, except the apostles. . . . As for Saul, he made havoc of the church, entering every house, and dragging off men and women, committing them to prison. (Acts 8:1, 3)

Saul gained letters of authority from the high priest and with demonic ferocity continued his vicious attacks. Then, miraculously, Jesus intervened on the road to Damascus.

> As he journeyed he came near Damascus, and suddenly a light shone around him from heaven. Then he fell to the ground, and heard a voice saying to him, "Saul, Saul, why are you persecuting Me?" And he said, "Who are You, Lord?" Then the Lord said, "I am Jesus, whom you are persecuting. It is hard for you to kick against the goads." (Acts 9:3–5)

Jesus' intervention in Saul's life reveals the marvelous depth of the mercy and kindness of God. Saul had done so much harm, not just to the disciples of the Lord but to the Lord Jesus Himself, who took Saul's actions personally: "I am Jesus, whom you are persecuting."

I am shocked that Jesus appealed to Saul based on how difficult *his* life became as he persecuted the church. Jesus asked him, "Isn't it hard for you to kick against the goads?" *Isn't it hard for you?* How amazing is the heart of God for every person!

Jesus had a profound destiny for this enemy of the gospel. He conscripted Ananias, a man of real faith, to rescue Saul. Ananias knew well Saul's reputation. But he overcame his apprehension, obeyed the Lord, found Saul, and restored his sight:

> And Ananias . . . laying his hands on him he said, "Brother Saul, the Lord Jesus, who appeared to you on the road as you came, has sent me that you may receive your sight and be filled with the Holy Spirit." Immediately there fell from his eyes something like scales, and he received his sight at once; and he arose and was baptized. So when he had received food, he was strengthened. Then Saul spent some days with the disciples at Damascus. Immediately he preached the Christ in the synagogues, that He is the Son of God. (Acts 9:17–20)

Who more than Paul is the prototype of one delivered from deserved consequences? He was not just a sinner. He sought the destruction of believers in Jesus and the very faith Jesus suffered and died to establish. The apostle Paul constantly proclaimed this marvelous grace. He wrote: "This is a faithful saying and worthy of all acceptance, that Christ Jesus came into the world to save sinners, of whom I am chief. However, for this reason I obtained mercy, that in me first Jesus Christ might show all longsuffering, as a pattern to those who are going to believe on Him for everlasting life" (1 Tim. 1:15–16).

The salvation of Saul of Tarsus is a primary example of how far the mercy of God is willing to reach. His mercy still reaches at least that far for anyone today.

THE IMPORTANCE OF GRACE

Grace has many manifestations but is most simply defined as "undeserved favor." To qualify for it you cannot deserve it. Grace is the only basis of deliverance available to us. It only comes as a gift. We must trust God to experience the fullness of His grace. Jeremiah wrote about the significance of trusting God:

Thus says the LORD:

"Cursed is the man who trusts in man
And makes flesh his strength,
Whose heart departs from the LORD.
For he shall be like a shrub in the desert,
And shall not see when good comes [KJV: see when good
        cometh],
But shall inhabit the parched places in the wilderness,
In a salt land which is not inhabited.

"Blessed is the man who trusts in the LORD,
And whose hope is the LORD.
For he shall be like a tree planted by the waters,
Which spreads out its roots by the river,

23

And will not fear when heat comes;
But its leaf will be green,
And will not be anxious in the year of drought,
Nor will cease from yielding fruit."

(JER. 17:5–8)

Jeremiah concluded that to trust ourselves is to put ourselves under a curse. The result is that we won't recognize good even when it comes. I have met people who first encountered Jesus and believed the gospel to the saving of their souls, but they turned from the grace of God to rely on their ability to keep the law for their justification. How tragic! It is a great deception to rely on obeying the Old Testament law to remain in fellowship with God. Paul the apostle confronted this heresy head-on: "You have become estranged from Christ, you who attempt to be justified by law; you have fallen from grace. . . . This persuasion does not come from Him who calls you" (Gal. 5:4, 8).

We must not let anything frustrate the Lord's prescribed way to deliver us from what we deserve.

Four

MUCH MORE THAN WE KNOW

Driving through the rolling hills of the North Carolina countryside, I rounded the bend and spotted a large hand-painted sign on the side of the road. In white letters it said, "To Go to Heaven When You Die, *You Must Be Born Again.*" Having grown up in the Bible Belt, I knew the sign expressed the prevailing belief about why one needs to be *born again*. Being born again delivers us from deserved consequences. It is God's prescribed way of forgiving and restoring us, and it secures our place in heaven when we die. But there is more to understand about it than that.

Jesus Himself introduced the born-again experience when He said to Nicodemus, "Most assuredly, I say to you, unless one is born again, he cannot see the kingdom of God" (John 3:3). To better clarify the meaning of being born again, Jesus gave a clue when He said, "He who comes from above is above all; he who is of the earth is earthly and speaks of the earth. He who comes from heaven is above all" (John 3:31). The word *above* is the same word translated "again," as in "born again," in verse 3. Jesus meant that one must be born from *above* (from heaven) by the agency of the Holy Spirit.

A primary purpose for being born from above is so that we can perceive and access heaven while we are alive. That may sound outrageous, but we must carefully consider the context of this conversation between Jesus and Nicodemus. Jesus was explaining to Nicodemus the source of His supernatural ministry. Because Jesus was born from heaven, He could see (perceive) and enter (access) the kingdom of God, as we shall see later, whenever He wanted to. He told Nicodemus that he, too, must be born from heaven to do the same.

CONTEXT: KEY TO UNDERSTANDING

If we assume we have complete understanding of a truth like being born again, we may no longer be open to further insight. Truth is often hidden in partial understanding and can be masked in plain sight. But if we look at the context in which being born again is introduced, we gain greater understanding.

After being filled with the Holy Spirit at His water baptism, Jesus of Nazareth startled the entire nation of Israel, including the Sanhedrin, by moving in unprecedented power, performing great miracles and signs. His baptism in the Spirit empowered His supernatural ministry as He perceived and accessed the kingdom of heaven. John's gospel describes the scope and breadth of Jesus' supernatural ministry:

> And truly Jesus did many other signs in the presence of His disciples, which are not written in this book; but these are written that you may believe that Jesus is the Christ, the Son of God, and that believing you may have life in His name. (John 20:30–31)

And there are also many other things that Jesus did, which if they were written one by one I suppose that even the world itself could not contain the books that would be written. Amen. (John 21:25)

The gospel accounts do not detail all Jesus did but present an approximate thirty-day snapshot of His ministry spread over three and a half years. The astounding number of healings and miracles Jesus demonstrated commanded the attention of the entire nation. Israel had never seen anything like it before. In the genesis of His ministry, no one knew who He was. He did not attend their schools in Jerusalem, was not a Levitical priest or a Pharisee, nor was He part of the Jewish elite. He was simply the carpenter from Nazareth. Leading into the conversation with Nicodemus, the Wuest Expanded Translation reveals how intensely Jesus was scrutinized: "Now, when He was in Jerusalem at the Passover Feast, many put their trust in His name, carefully observing with a purposeful interest and a critical and a discerning eye, His attesting miracles which He was constantly performing" (John 2:23 WET).

NICODEMUS AND JESUS

Nicodemus was one of those who carefully observed with amazement and wonder all Jesus was doing. He was a prominent ruler of the Jews and a primary judge on the Jewish Sanhedrin. As part of the body of ruling elders, his responsibility was to judge the orthodoxy of anyone who could lead the people astray. He came to examine up close this Galilean miracle worker. Nicodemus must have wondered how Jesus could do all He was doing. He would soon find out!

In the exchange between Jesus and Nicodemus (John 3:1–21), Nicodemus came to Jesus with a question. Jesus discerned

Nicodemus's heart and began to answer even before the Jewish ruler could ask. To understand Jesus' answer we must first understand what Nicodemus *did not* ask. He did not ask, "Jesus, how can I know I will go to heaven when I die?" That is the question many twenty-first-century believers assume Jesus answered. But from the context of the encounter and the substance of Jesus' response, Nicodemus wanted to understand *how* Jesus could constantly do such amazing miracles.

Nicodemus's introductory remarks began, "Rabbi, we *know* that You are a teacher come from God; for no one can do these signs that You do unless God is with him" (John 3:2). Jesus quickly responded, "Most assuredly, I say to you, unless one is born again, he cannot *see* the kingdom of God" (v. 3).

I italicized the words *know* and *see* in the scriptures above to emphasize that they are the exact same word *eido*, translated in the text two different ways in these two consecutive verses. *Eido* means "to see, to perceive with the eyes, or to perceive by any of the senses." In this context it means "to perceive, discern, or discover." Therefore, to *see* the kingdom of God is to perceive it.

When I was in college studying mathematics I sometimes struggled to understand certain concepts and theories. At a given point I would suddenly perceive the meaning and say to myself, *Oh, now I see!* That is the sense of the word *see* in this conversation. It means "to perceive." Until you perceive the kingdom you will not access it.

Nicodemus said, "We [*perceive*] that You are a teacher come from God; for no one can do these signs that You do unless God is with him." Jesus immediately responded, in effect, "Nicodemus, you cannot [*perceive*] the realm of the kingdom of God unless you are born again from heaven."

Nicodemus's sarcastic response revealed his frustration with

Jesus' answer. He asked, "Can he enter a second time into his mother's womb and be born?" (v. 4). Ignoring Nicodemus's frustration Jesus stayed on point and continued to answer the deeper issue He wanted Nicodemus to understand. Jesus replied, "Most assuredly, I say to you, unless one is born of water and the Spirit, he cannot enter the kingdom of God" (v. 5).

To perceive the kingdom of God and to enter or access it, Jesus said we must be born from that realm.

Why Born of Water?

Jesus said one must be born both of water and the Spirit to access the kingdom of God. Being born of water refers to natural childbirth, the way a person enters the earth realm. The birth is normally preceded by the breaking of the mother's aqueous membrane that releases a flow of water. Being born of water doesn't refer to baptism. Baptism in water is for believers, not something that makes a nonbeliever a Christian.

One must first be born of water, born into the earth realm to be legitimately eligible to be born again by the Spirit of God to access the heavenly realm. Being born from those two dimensions makes us eligible to exercise authority over the demonic realm. Neither the devil nor demons are born here and have no authority here unless they gain control of the authority we have. From the very beginning in the garden of Eden, Satan intended to (and successfully) usurped Adam's authority on the earth.

For the same reason, Jesus was born here to regain legitimate authority here. By virtue of Jesus' conception by the Holy Spirit, He was both born here *and* was from above, making Him eligible to reclaim as a man the authority Adam lost. After we are born into this realm, we must be born again from the heavenly one to have the spiritual capacity and legitimate authority to righteously access the heavenly realm.

Jesus then made a point with astounding implications. He said, "The wind blows where it wishes, and you hear the sound of it, but cannot tell where it comes from and where it goes. So is everyone who is born of the Spirit" (John 3:8). Pay close attention to what He actually said. He taught that a *person* born from above by the Spirit is like the wind in that he can go where he wants. Once again, understand what Jesus meant in the context of this conversation. A person who is born again can go where he wants, in the context of perceiving and accessing the kingdom of God.

The wind blows where it wishes. Jesus said that anyone born of the Spirit can do the same thing. The word *wishes* means "to will, to determine as an active option from a subjective impulse." Some assume the verse means that the Holy Spirit *blows* you where He wants you to go, but that is not what Jesus said. He did not say we are like kites that the wind blows; He said that, like the wind, we can go where we want. He said that if you are born of the Spirit you can perceive the kingdom of God and access, or *go into*, the kingdom of God when *you* want to. It's not a geographical going but a spiritual one. Jesus explained to Nicodemus how He did supernatural things: by perceiving and accessing the kingdom of God. The wind goes where it wants. He, being born of the Spirit, did too. And so can you if you are born again.

Jesus taught that we "hear the sound of [the wind], but cannot tell where it comes from and where it goes" (John 3:8). You see and hear the effects of the wind, but you do not see the wind itself. The same is true of one born of the Spirit. You can sit in plain view of everyone, close your eyes and pray, or by faith access the resources of the kingdom of God and release the power of God. In essence, you go in by faith and come back with an impartation, but no one saw you go. If in fact you have done it, people will get healed, you will have a prophetic word, or you may release something wonderful to someone *here* by perceiving and accessing something from *there*. We are like the wind.

Some might argue that my conclusions are unrealistic, impossible, or—perhaps more seriously—that they are false. They might conclude that if it were true, everyone who is born again would do it, but since they do not, it must not be true.

Consider that during the Dark Ages justification by faith was hidden for more than a thousand years. What was possible and accessible was no longer experienced because so few knew it was available and therefore did not believe unto justification. It was hidden, but after Martin Luther and other Reformers recovered the truth of justification by faith, the entire world benefited from the impact of that simple truth. Everywhere that message traveled, people were saved, born again, and millions of lives were changed.

I grew up in a spiritual tradition that did not believe in the prophetic ministry as we know it today. For that reason I never had prophetic words nor saw examples of that kind of ministry. After I was born again and filled with the Spirit, I began to believe I could do what the early church did and began to have sporadic prophetic words for people. I struggled to function in that ministry but persisted in believing in the truth of it. I received prophetic words and encounters in an almost capricious and random way.

Years later I realized I could receive words from Him whenever I asked for them and access them by faith. What I once assumed was not possible was possible. As my faith and understanding increased, so did my experiences. The apostle Paul wrote, "You can all prophesy one by one, that all may learn and all may be encouraged" (1 Cor. 14:31) and that we "prophesy in proportion to our faith" (Rom. 12:6).

How does it work? Let me first say I believe that God heals people today and that He wants to use us to do it. Does everyone I pray for get healed? No, but more people I pray for get healed than when I ignore them and don't pray. In other words, in every aspect of spiritual giftedness there is a learning process. It takes faith, insight, persistence, and a good fight of faith to recover the highest effective levels of prophetic functionality, even though it is readily available to all believers.

The Bible reveals that even Jesus prayed twice for one particular man to completely receive his sight (Mark 8:22–25). At other times the prevailing state of unbelief or the heart condition of those He ministered to restricted His miracle ministry (Mark 6:5–6). The real issue is whether or not we believe our beliefs and how much we are willing to fight for what we can have. Our failure rate is no indicator of the validity or availability of this level of spiritual dynamic. How badly we want it may be a more accurate explanation for our lack of success.

The crux of entering the realm of the heavens is to a large degree contingent on our faith and will to persevere. It doesn't happen automatically. Jesus used the wind as His primary example of accessing the heavens saying, "The wind goes where it wills." How strong is your will to do it? How determined are you to apprehend the thing that you have been apprehended by Christ Jesus to do (Phil. 3:12)?

We find another interesting example in Romans: "Through whom also we have access by faith into this grace in which we stand, and rejoice in hope of the glory of God" (5:2).

We can stand in a grace that we do not always access. We cannot earn it. It has been given to us, but to access it we must exercise our faith through Him. Certain aspects of the spiritual life are not automatic. If they were, Paul would not have exhorted us to "pursue love, and desire spiritual gifts" (1 Cor. 14:1). That's the "more excellent way," to pursue the realm of the Spirit with love so that we can help those who need it (1 Cor. 12:31).

LIVING A BILOCATIONAL LIFE

Jesus continued in His encounter with Nicodemus and said, "No one has ascended to heaven but He who came down from heaven, that is, the Son of Man who is in heaven" (John 3:13).

As a man, Jesus lived a "bilocational" life. In essence He simultaneously held dual citizenship, on earth and in heaven. This may seem to be an outlandish statement; nevertheless, it is true. But what is more astonishing is that you have the capacity to live the same kind of life: *on earth and in heaven* at the same time. Jesus came to show us not how God would live if He came to earth but how men could live who were born again. What else did Paul mean when he said that God has "raised us up together, and made us sit together in the heavenly places in Christ Jesus" (Eph. 2:6)? Paul's statement is more than a doctrinal position. It must be practically demonstrated.

When Jesus was filled with the Holy Spirit, His Father empowered Him, enabling Him to demonstrate to the world what a person could do who perceived and accessed the kingdom of God. We, too, must experience the infilling of the Holy Spirit to move in the fullness of our potential. It is possible to be equipped and yet not be fully empowered. The apostles and disciples healed people and cast out demons before being empowered with the Holy Spirit at Pentecost. After their encounter with the Holy Spirit in the Upper Room, however, they became exponentially more effective when more than three thousand fellow Jews came to Christ (Acts 2:41).

"YOU MUST BE BORN AGAIN"

"You must be born again" has to be more than a warning to those who are not yet saved or the rallying cry of fundamental Christians. Being born again must become in each of us a basic understanding of why we are given new life and of the possibilities God entrusted to us. People's destinies, health, and very lives hang in the balance.

We have a new day before us rife with huge possibilities. Now is the time to arise and shine. Our light has come, and the Lord Himself wants to arise upon us in unprecedented ways. It is time for the next Great Awakening.

What about you? Are you committed to seeing His kingdom come in your life, in your family, in your city, and in your nation? To be able to change society is part of your birthright. Jesus died so that we could access the heavens and release the goodness of God everywhere we go. Don't turn away from this great calling. As said Hillel the elder, a prominent first-century rabbi, I charge you: "If not you, who? If not now, when?"

Part Three

WAGON TWO: DELIVERANCE FROM CRITICISM AND THE CRITICAL SPIRIT

Five

DESTROYER OF HOPE

Criticism is a major enemy of hope. It impedes the development of a person's identity by giving us an inaccurate understanding of who we are. That false understanding hinders the ability to fulfill one's destiny. Wagon number two of my vision contained *deliverance from criticism and the critical spirit.*

As I grew up, kids in the neighborhood hurt one other by saying cruel things. Wounded kids responded with that tired old adage, "Sticks and stones may break my bones but words shall never harm me," shouting over their shoulders as they left for home wounded from the insults. That adage wasn't true then, and it's not true now. Words have power to harm or to heal, to build up or to tear down. Critical words, particularly from a person of influence and authority can be devastating. Criticism's poison infects many people, and God wants to deliver every one of them.

The danger with being criticized is that thoughts become strongholds that bind and control us. It affects us much like the method captors use to train and control elephants. Men have used the great animals for centuries to haul lumber, harvest crops, even transport weapons and soldiers into battle. Their strength is legendary. An average mature African bull, the largest of the surviving land animals, weighs nineteen thousand pounds. The largest elephant on record, shot in Angola in 1955, weighed more than twenty-six thousand pounds, stood more than thirteen feet tall at the shoulder, and was thirty-three feet long. A preserved version sits on display at the Smithsonian Institution in the Natural History Museum.

A Small Chain, a Large Stronghold

How do men dominate beasts so much larger and stronger than they are? They start with a small chain and a strong stake when the young elephant is small. The captor chains his leg to a wooden peg securely planted in the ground. At first the elephant struggles to escape but quickly realizes he is no match for the chain that binds him and soon stops struggling to get free. His experience conditions him to believe his chain will always be stronger than he is. The same chain that restrained him when he weighed two hundred pounds now imprisons him when he weighs nineteen thousand pounds. The elephant that carries heavy loads, pulls trees out of the earth, and harvests thousands of pounds of lumber is held captive by a chain attached to a stake that any normal man could pull from the ground. It is not the chain around his ankle that binds him; it's the chain inside his mind.

The elephant's bondage began as a physical one but became much more powerful as a stronghold in his mind. Criticism can control people in much the same way. Like the trained elephant, many people are bound mentally and spiritually by *believing* the misguided words spoken to them. The strength of that bondage lies in direct proportion to how much they believe those critical words.

Criticism can distort a person's identity. Just like the chain that holds the elephant in fear and bondage, evil negative words hold people captive by imposing an inaccurate concept of who they are. Many need deliverance from those word curses into a true knowledge of how God feels about them. He alone gives us an accurate understanding of our true identity. We must agree with Him and declare what He declares about us.

The wagons in my encounter speak prophetically to this vital truth. They were ancient ones, constructed with wooden spoked wheels and pulled by a handle called the tongue. God, in His economy, filled these ancient wagons with provision generations before we needed it. The *spoken* wheels and *tongue* speak of the practical way we access their provision. We believe in, agree with, and proclaim with our mouths the truth they represent.

The words we speak are so important, especially when they are spoken in faith. The apostle Paul said, "With the heart one believes unto righteousness, and with the mouth confession is made unto salvation" (Rom. 10:10). Solomon's proverb reinforces this truth: "Death and life are in the power of the tongue, and those who love it will eat its fruit" (Prov. 18:21). In both references our proclamation brings salvation and bears fruit. It is so important to see from heaven's perspective and speak over our lives and others' lives words that build and encourage rather than destroy and tear down.

IDENTITY LEADING TO DESTINY: JOHN THE BAPTIST

Knowing who God created us to be is foundational to fulfilling our destiny. A battle rages over each of us as the enemy of our souls tries to confuse us with a false identity and keep us from our purpose. The birth of John the Baptist and his father's encounter with God's angel give us insight into discovering who God created us to be.

Luke introduced the aging priest Zacharias, a man with a long, unfulfilled desire to have a son. His old age and his wife Elizabeth's barrenness made it impossible (Luke 1:5–7).

We meet Zacharias when his turn arose to officiate in the temple at the altar of incense. It is likely the only time in his life he was honored to do so. The job of the priest was to burn incense on the altar continually. The rising smoke symbolized the prayers of God's people ascending to heaven. As he attended the altar an angel suddenly appeared and frightened Zacharias. The heavenly messenger delivered an amazing promise:

> The angel said to him, "Do not be afraid, Zacharias, for your prayer is heard; and your wife Elizabeth will bear you a son, and you shall call his name John. And you will have joy and gladness, and many will rejoice at his birth. For he will be great in the sight of the Lord, and shall drink neither wine nor strong drink. He will also be filled with the Holy Spirit, even from his mother's womb. And he will turn many of the children of Israel to the Lord their God. He will also go before Him in the spirit and power of Elijah, 'to turn the hearts of the fathers to the children,' and the disobedient to the wisdom of the just, to make ready a people prepared for the Lord." (Luke 1:13–17)

The phrase "your prayer has been heard" can be translated as "the prayer you don't even pray anymore" (John 1:13, footnote TPT). Some prayers remain alive in heaven long after we have given up on their fulfillment. They have a longer shelf life than our faith does. Many prayers will only be answered at the most strategic time. It is God's desire to answer, but Father knows best. God intended to answer the heart cries of Zacharias and Elizabeth in the person of John the Baptist, who would change the course of human history.

The angel's announcement shocked Zacharias. Would God truly fulfill the deepest prayer of his heart? Yes, but He would refrain until the most strategic time to do so. Then heaven named the child John, decreeing his identity and preparing him in his mother's womb. Zacharias panicked and responded in an unacceptable way, setting in motion a most unusual sequence of events:

> Zacharias said to the angel, "How shall I know this? For I am an old man, and my wife is well advanced in years." And the angel answered and said to him, "I am Gabriel, who stands in the presence of God, and was sent to speak to you and bring you these glad tidings. But behold, you will be mute and not able to speak until the day these things take place, because you did not believe my words which will be fulfilled in their own time." (Luke 1:18–20)

Zacharias didn't believe Gabriel, one of the Lord's most authoritative messengers. But the angel made the priest unable to speak until the birth of the child. It may have been the mercy of God that the angel silenced him so he couldn't negate the promise through speaking his deeply held unbelief. Solomon wrote, "Death and life are in the power of the tongue, and those who love it will eat its fruit" (Prov. 18:21), for good or bad. Zacharias's inability to speak continually reminded him that the angel's word was true and that the miraculous fulfillment of his promise was imminent.

Zacharias emerged from the temple as a mute. Meanwhile, the miracle power of God enabled Elizabeth to conceive. As her belly grew, the birth of young John became apparent to all: "Now after those days his wife Elizabeth conceived; and she hid herself five months, saying, 'Thus the Lord has dealt with me, in the days when He looked on me, to take away my reproach among people'" (Luke 1:24–25).

Prior to the birth of the child, Elizabeth's cousin Mary visited her. I am sure Elizabeth's miracle conception greatly encouraged Mary. She had an even more amazing heavenly encounter, for inside her womb grew the most profound and greatest miracle. She, too, was pregnant but without the aid of natural human conception. Three months after Mary's visit, Elizabeth gave birth to her dear child, and God removed the years of her reproach.

Initially, Zacharias doubted Gabriel's message, but after his nine-month exile of silence and Elizabeth's pregnancy, he doubted no longer. Finally the child was born.

> So it was, on the eighth day, that they came to circumcise the child; and they would have called him by the name of his father, Zacharias. His mother answered and said, "No; he shall be called John." But they said to her, "There is no one among your relatives who is called by this name." So they made signs to his father—what he would have him called. (Luke 1:59–62)

The family insisted that the child be named after his father, but Elizabeth would have none of it. They appealed to Zacharias to ensure the child bore his name. "And he asked for a writing tablet, and wrote, saying, 'His name is John.' So they all marveled. Immediately his mouth was opened and his tongue loosed, and he spoke, praising God" (vv. 63–64).

After nine silent months the first words Zacharias spoke were, "His name is John." Heaven had prevailed.

TRADITIONS

It is amazing how strong traditions can be. They are certainly not all bad, but when they contradict the mind of the Lord they should be ignored. Heaven determined the birth of this child, and heaven maintained the right to name him. Tradition intended to make the child conform into its own image. Our enemy uses criticism in much the same way, to shape us into an inaccurate understanding of who we are.

John was called to be a person unlike anyone from Zacharias's family. John was a unique man with a unique calling. He was actually filled with the Holy Spirit while in his mother's womb. He needed to be named accurately to fulfill his identity. John's name means "Jehovah is a gracious giver." What more profound name than that should the child be given who would prepare the nation and the world for their Savior, God's ultimate gift? Thank God, Elizabeth and Zacharias held their ground. We must hold our ground as well when it comes to our own identity.

Zacharias regained his voice when he agreed with the counsel of heaven. We must heed that vital truth. Many have lost their voice by allowing tradition, the good intentions of those around them, or criticism, to unduly influence them, pervert their identity, and short-circuit their destiny.

Why should John bear his father's name? He had a unique and completely different calling. Zacharias, whose name means "God has remembered," couldn't live up to his name himself. He didn't believe God remembered him. He argued with the angel of the Lord, who promised him God was about to answer his deepest prayer, even as the entire encounter happened at the altar of incense, the most profound symbol of prayer in all Judaism.

Too many times fathers try to live out their own unfulfilled dreams through their sons, which can rob the sons of their own unique destinies. We cannot live subject to others' opinions, yield to traditions contrary to our purpose, or allow criticism to keep us from fulfilling God's destiny for our lives.

A Precious Heritage

I honor and deeply appreciate my family heritage, having come from a long line of strong, godly Christians of at least six generations. I would not be the person I am today apart from that heritage. My forefathers sailed to America before the Revolutionary War to escape religious persecution. They paid a precious price to practice religious freedom that the New World offered them. But when I met the Lord, He began something in my life that fell outside the spiritual tradition that raised me. Jesus baptized me in the Holy Spirit and I spoke in tongues. That was not normal in my church tradition.

I yearned for and began to experience the supernatural kind of life I saw in the New Testament. I experienced valuable and unusual encounters with the Lord, began functioning in prophetic ministry, had amazing dreams, and saw God move in healing and in legitimate signs and wonders. My original tribe couldn't relate to my experience. To them it was a road less traveled, and some considered it heretical. Sometimes I didn't understand my journey either but instinctively knew as a young man I must continue walking the road the Lord set before me.

I remember family reunions with my believing relatives. As we shared our meals together, my cousins, some who were pastors, asked me what I was doing. When I told them I pastored a church, they asked where I went to seminary. After I told them I hadn't gone to seminary, one said, "Then you can't be a pastor!" I replied, "Okay . . . pass the fried chicken; please."

I didn't expect them to understand, and I didn't go to the family reunion to ask them who I was. I knew. They wanted to name me after my *fathers*, and I understood why. That was what they knew. But God had begun revealing to me my true identity. That was sufficient for me.

Six

KNOW WHO YOU ARE

Criticism cannot define us when we know who we are, when we see ourselves as God sees us. Only the Lord can reveal our true identity to us. As we grow into the fullness of that revelation, we become a force to be reckoned with.

Simon Bar-Jonah, one of the Lord's greatest apostles, did not know who he really was until he met Jesus. Jesus walked Simon through a process of discovery that began at their introduction when Jesus nicknamed him Peter, meaning "rock," as a foreshadowing of who he would become. Simon knew himself to be a brother, a husband, and a fisherman whose forefathers learned their trade on the Sea of Galilee. Jesus knew Simon to be a foundational man destined to help establish a spiritual movement to release heaven's kingdom on earth. This heavenly kingdom would ultimately dismantle and replace every other kingdom of this world.

In the New Testament Jesus addressed Simon Bar-Jonah as Peter only five times. Each time He used this name, Jesus revealed to Simon more of his true identity.

One of the two who heard John speak, and followed Him, was Andrew, Simon Peter's brother. He first found his own brother Simon, and said to him, "We have found the Messiah" (which is translated, the Christ). And he brought him to Jesus. Now when Jesus looked at him, He said, "You are Simon the son of Jonah. You shall be called Cephas" (which is translated, A Stone). (John 1:40–42)

This passage describes the first meeting of Jesus and Simon Bar-Jonah. In His introductory conversation Jesus prophesied to Simon, giving him a new name that had implications much greater than the fisherman could imagine. The text uses the name Cephas, the Aramaic form for Peter, meaning "a stone." And such a stone, a living stone, Simon Son of Jonah would become. In effect, Jesus was saying, "I know who you are, but you don't. You are Peter, a rock!" Jesus began to unravel Simon's old identity and plant revelatory seeds of his true identity that would sprout and grow as his relationship with Jesus developed.

Jesus called Simon by his new name, Peter, the second time in the midst of a pivotal conversation. He didn't use the name haphazardly. Nothing Jesus said or did was without purpose.

When Jesus came into the region of Caesarea Philippi, He asked His disciples, saying, "Who do men say that I, the Son of Man, am?"

So they said, "Some say John the Baptist, some Elijah, and others Jeremiah or one of the prophets."

He said to them, "But who do you say that I am?"

Simon Peter answered and said, "You are the Christ, the Son of the living God."

Jesus answered and said to him, "Blessed are you, Simon

Bar-Jonah, for flesh and blood has not revealed this to you, but My Father who is in heaven. And I also say to you that you are Peter, and on this rock I will build My church, and the gates of Hades shall not prevail against it. And I will give you the keys of the kingdom of heaven, and whatever you bind on earth will be bound in heaven, and whatever you loose on earth will be loosed in heaven." (Matt. 16:13–19)

The meaning of Jesus' declaration to Peter—"You are *Peter*, and on this rock I will build My church, and the gates of Hades shall not prevail against it" (v. 18)—has been debated for centuries. Protestants and Catholics have very differing views. In simplicity the Roman Catholic interpretation is one of "apostolic succession": the church is built on Peter, the first pope, and each succeeding pope ordained down through the ages. Most Protestants believe the church is built on the rock of revelation—Jesus is the Christ—which is true, but there is more also.

The gates of Hades *have* prevailed against both Catholic *and* Protestant churches. How many folks from both persuasions do you know who are oppressed by sickness, poverty, disease, depression, the evil influence of Satan himself, whose job description is to *steal*, *kill*, and *destroy* (John 10:10)? Believers in both camps *may* know Jesus as the Christ, and yet they do not prevail against the gates of Hades!

We must understand what Jesus meant when He proclaimed that He is building a church upon which the "gates of Hades" would have no effect. Hades, the abode of the dead, is the personification of death, and represents the demonic forces behind sin and ruin. City gates were primary access points that protected each city. Men of authority sat at these gates and determined who and what could enter the city.

People are like gates, being access points to others by influencing people for good or evil. The gates of Hades are a prophetic picture of people who have become access points for death and the power of the enemy. They often release death through the critical and even evil words they speak. Any one of us can be used that way if we are not careful. Peter himself once became that kind of access point when he rebuked Jesus for proclaiming His impending death; Jesus even called him Satan: "Then Peter took Him aside and began to rebuke Him, saying, 'Far be it from You, Lord; this shall not happen to You!' But He turned and said to Peter, 'Get behind Me, Satan! You are an offense to Me, for you are not mindful of the things of God, but the things of men'" (Matt. 16:22–23).

Jesus identified some Pharisees as gates of Hades as well when He said, "But woe to you, scribes and Pharisees, hypocrites! For you shut up the kingdom of heaven against men; for you neither go in yourselves, nor do you allow those who are entering to go in" (Matt. 23:13).

Jesus rebuked scribes and Pharisees for closing the kingdom of heaven to men, because like gates they stood in the way of people's access to the kingdom and were unwilling to enter themselves.

What then is this church that can prevail over the gates of Hades? It is a church comprised of people who know who Jesus is and who *they* are as revealed to them by Christ Jesus. In essence, Jesus told Simon, "Now that you know who I am, I can tell you who you are!" We cannot know our God-given identity apart from Him, our Creator. And we can't fully know who we are until we can tell Him who He is. This dual revelation is the rock Jesus referred to. When someone like Peter knows both these things, he becomes a rock against whom the gates of Hades will not prevail.

THE CHURCH FOUNDED ON THIS ROCK

Scripture confirms the idea of the rock upon which the church is built:

> Now, therefore, you are no longer strangers and foreigners, but fellow citizens with the saints and members of the household of God, having been built on the foundation of the apostles and prophets, Jesus Christ Himself being the chief cornerstone, in whom the whole building, being fitted together, grows into a holy temple in the Lord, in whom you also are being built together for a dwelling place of God in the Spirit. (Eph. 2:19–22)

Paul began these verses by reminding the Ephesian believers of their true identity: "no longer strangers and foreigners, but fellow citizens with the saints and members of the household of God." The habitation of God is built on knowing who we are as we live together on the foundation of the apostles and prophets, who knew who they were, with the cornerstone being Christ Himself, who certainly knew who He was. Jesus said, "On *this* rock I will build My church, and the gates of Hades shall not prevail against it" (Matt. 16:18).

Unwitting people who are influenced by the spirit of this age have no power over those who have discovered their God-given identities. At the same time we must heed these words of the apostle Paul: "We do not wrestle against flesh and blood, but against principalities, against powers, against the rulers of the darkness of this age, against spiritual hosts of wickedness in the heavenly places" (Eph. 6:12).

People are not our enemies; the devil is. People are only the gates through which the enemy tries to prevail. But believers who are well established in their own God-given identities and know Jesus Christ will prevail against all the influence of people who are dominated by the evil one.

Jesus referred to His impulsive Galilean friend as *Peter* for the third time in the context of Simon's impending public humiliation. This time Jesus revealed His grace and unwavering personal commitment to Peter no matter what he might do:

> And the Lord said, "Simon, Simon! Indeed, Satan has asked for you, that he may sift you as wheat. But I have prayed for you, that your faith should not fail; and when you have returned to Me, strengthen your brethren."
>
> But he said to Him, "Lord, I am ready to go with You, both to prison and to death."
>
> Then He said, "I tell you, Peter, the rooster shall not crow this day before you will deny three times that you know Me." (Luke 22:31–34)

Through this exchange with Jesus, Peter stepped into the most humiliating days of his life. Within hours or perhaps even minutes, he denied the Lord whom he loved with all his heart. He thought he could withstand ultimate adversity, but he wasn't yet prepared. Peter did not fully know his true identity.

Jesus accepted Simon, affirmed Simon, loved him through the worst day of his life, the day he denied the Lord. Satan sorely sifted Simon Bar-Jonah, but after the chaff fell from the wheat of his life, *Peter* remained.

Redemptive Failure

Jesus used Peter's failure, one the apostle brought upon himself through his pride, to put to death this part of his old nature that could keep him from fulfilling his destiny. If he had agreed with Jesus' assessment, Peter could have avoided this fall, but since his pride had so deceived him, it became unavoidable. He learned in a profound way he could not trust in himself to fulfill the assignment Jesus appointed him to. He must fully lean on the Lord.

How about you? Have you failed the Lord, gone down in flames, utterly embarrassed and humiliated yourself? It is not too late for you to return to Him in a way that will make you stronger than ever before. Jesus, knowing of Peter's impending failure, told him to strengthen his brethren when he was converted.

God can use your failure to cause you to stop trusting in yourself and enable you to strengthen those around you. It is certainly not the best way to learn life's lessons; nevertheless, the Lord will redeem our failures if we let Him. If after your worst, most humiliating experience in life, all you have left to rely on is Jesus and His love, then you have truly found the best part. Peter did and you can too. His best, most glorious days were still before him. Yours may be too.

After the resurrection, Jesus referred to Simon as *Peter* a fourth time (Mark 16:6–8). While Jesus Himself did not say Peter's name, his authorized messenger did so on His behalf:

> "Do not be alarmed. You seek Jesus of Nazareth, who was crucified. He is risen! He is not here. See the place where they laid Him. But go, tell His disciples—and Peter—that He is going before you into

Galilee; there you will see Him, as He said to you." So they went out quickly and fled from the tomb, for they trembled and were amazed. And they said nothing to anyone, for they were afraid. (Mark 16:6–8)

Peter's cowardly betrayal of Jesus left the once bold apostle utterly discouraged. Perhaps he felt like he would never recover the faith and courage he had in his earlier walk with Jesus. *That* Peter was the only apostle who walked on water and the only one who attacked the crowd that took Jesus prisoner. Maybe the other leaders also concluded that Peter failed so horribly that Jesus would never trust him again. But the opposite was true. His best, most courageous days were not behind him but in his immediate future and beyond.

The angel instructed the women at the tomb to "go, tell His disciples—and Peter" and go to Galilee, for there they would see the risen Jesus. It is significant that this phrase appears only in the gospel of Mark. That gospel is known as "Peter's gospel," written from the perspective of John Mark, Peter's adopted spiritual son. Those two words "and Peter" meant more to Simon Bar-Jonah than anyone could know.

By addressing Simon as *Peter* this fourth time, I can imagine Jesus tenderly saying, "Peter, you may have forgotten who you are but I never did. I knew what you would do since the first day I met you. You may have failed Me, but I know who you are, who you will become, and what I have for you to do for My name's sake. Others counted you out. You did, too, but I never for a minute gave up on you!"

Jesus' affirmation and acceptance of Peter after his fall became a watershed moment for the apostle. He would forever know the love of Jesus who accepted him and stood by him in his darkest hour. He would also know he could not trust himself but must fully rely on the Lord.

Acts 10 reveals the fifth time in Scripture that Jesus addressed Simon as *Peter*. The story revolves around the life of Cornelius, a Roman centurion who captured the Lord's attention by his generosity and personal devotion. The Lord sent an angel to tell Cornelius of a man named Peter that he must meet. The angel said that Peter was staying in Joppa with Simon the tanner in a house by the sea. In obedience to the angel's instruction, Cornelius sent a trusted soldier and two servants to find this important man.

Meanwhile, the next day Peter went up on the housetop and prayed. He became hungry and fell into a trance, when he saw heaven open and a large sheet come down. The sheet contained all kinds of animals that were unlawful for a devout Jew to eat.

PETER'S DILEMMA

Up to this point in church history, our forefathers did not understand that Jesus' sacrifice was intended to save others as well as the Jewish nation. The apostle Peter was unaware of the Lord's intention to bring the Gentiles into the kingdom of God. But Jesus initiated a foolproof plan to help Peter make the transition. While Peter was praying *and hungry*, the Lord lowered a sheet full of animals that were unclean, according to their ancient tradition and commands.

The Lord said, "Rise, Peter; kill and eat" (Acts 10:13). That sheet was a strange new menu lowered from heaven for the hungry apostle. When Peter refused the fare, as any good Jew would, the Lord responded, "What God has cleansed you must not call common" (v. 15). Three times the Lord repeated the process.

While Peter considered the meaning of this extraordinarily perplexing encounter, the Holy Spirit spoke to him, saying, "Behold, three men are seeking you. Arise therefore, go down and go with them, doubting nothing; for I have sent them" (vv. 19–20).

Three visions, three sheets of unclean animals, three times the Lord saying the animals were clean enough to eat, and three Gentiles at Peter's door asking specifically for him! The Lord directed him to go with them and doubt nothing, for He Himself sent them. Peter went with them to Cornelius's house, where he preached the gospel to them. And the Holy Spirit came too: "Those of the circumcision who believed were astonished, as many as came with Peter, because the gift of the Holy Spirit had been poured out on the Gentiles also. For they heard them speak with tongues and magnify God" (vv. 45–46).

Speaking in tongues was the confirming sign that Gentiles could be saved. Because they heard them do so and magnify the Lord, Peter baptized the new Gentile believers, and a new era of church history began. Jesus addressed Simon Bar-Jonah as *Peter* this fifth time to show him that to fulfill his calling he *must* be willing to change his mind about some significant things or he would never enter into the fullness of this new identity and fulfill the destiny God had for him.

Are you ready to change your mind? If you are going to go the distance to fulfill your calling and fully embrace your identity, you will certainly be challenged to change your mind and line up with heaven's perspective. How many believers have sacrificed their ultimate destinies and callings because they weren't prepared to take big risks and make significant changes? How many of us have allowed tradition and the fear of man to keep us from God's best for our lives?

Peter accepted the challenge and made the necessary changes, even in the face of his Jewish brethren's misunderstanding of his actions that day in Cornelius's house. Peter obeyed the Lord and opened the door to the kingdom of God for the rest of the world to enter.

Keys of the Kingdom

When Jesus revealed to Peter his true identity, He also gave him keys to opening the kingdom of heaven:

> And now I'm going to tell you who you are, *really* are. You are Peter, a rock. This is the rock on which I will put together my church, a church so expansive with energy that not even the gates of hell will be able to keep it out.
>
> And that's not all. You will have complete and free access to God's kingdom, keys to open any and every door: no more barriers between heaven and earth, earth and heaven. A yes on earth is yes in heaven. A no on earth is no in heaven. (Matt. 16:18–19 THE MESSAGE)

The keys to Peter's authority on earth lay in his agreement with heaven. And it is the same with us who allow Jesus to establish our true identities. A simple *yes* or *no*—the keys of agreement—have power to open every door.

In the process of discovering his identity, Peter opened two doors to the kingdom of heaven: one for his countrymen, the Jews at Pentecost, and the other for the Gentiles. In Simon the tanner's house Peter said, "Not so, Lord!" when Jesus first told him to kill and eat the animals on the sheet. As long as Peter said *no* when Jesus was saying *yes*, God's purpose was thwarted. *No agreement, no keys available.* But when Peter agreed with Jesus' assessment and said *yes*, he *unlocked* heaven's door to all Gentiles, and Cornelius and his whole household were saved and filled with the Holy Spirit. The gates of Hades no longer prevailed against the one called Peter when he agreed with heaven.

Peter knew from his youth that he was a fisherman. And he was a fisherman, but not the kind Jesus called him to be. He thought he was more courageous than the other apostles, but he found out he was not. Thankfully, Jesus had enough courage for both of them when Peter stayed in union with Him. Until Simon Bar-Jonah met Jesus he did not know who he was. But afterward he became a man Jesus could use to change the course of world history. God delivered him from every evil word and crippling experience that bound him to being less than the man he was created and called to be: Peter, the rock.

Seven

To Be and to Do

Two key components to our identities are our *relational identity*—who we are relative to God and His love—and our *functional identity*—what we are assigned to do. During the last forty-five years of my Christian life I have encountered the Lord in ways that helped me step into both aspects of my identity.

My Relational Identity

Sad to say, I was a Christian for more than a decade before I had a profound personal knowledge of God's love for me. Before then if someone asked if I knew that God loved me, of course I would have said *yes*. But that's not the same thing as knowing it, deeply knowing it. One morning as I awoke in that halfway state between sleep and consciousness, the Lord silently whispered to me: *Each one of My children is My own personal favorite.* That dear sentiment from the Lord got my attention. Could it be that I am God's favorite person? He then continued, *But very few people believe it.*

Everyone is not my favorite person. I don't have the capacity to love everyone that way, but God does. He loves each one of us as if we are His only one. How great is our God! The psalmist knew how God felt about him when he wrote,

> How precious also are Your thoughts to me, O God!
> How great is the sum of them!
> If I should count them, they would be more in number than the sand;
> When I awake, I am still with You.
>
> (Ps. 139:17–18)

These verses lend themselves to a profound truth for one who has experienced a true *spiritual awakening*. It is the continual experience of the presence and kindness of God.

On a different morning I heard that same quiet voice of the Lord say, *I think about you all the time.* Each of us is constantly on His mind. Life certainly has its share of tragedies, but what could be more tragic than to live your entire life as God's favorite person and not know it? How many of us are profoundly aware that He thinks of us all the time in a loving way? *You* are God's favorite person. When you realize that, you are well on your way to comprehending who you really are.

One day after preaching a not so good message, I sensed dissatisfaction and rejection from those who heard me. I wasn't happy with my message that day either. I consoled myself by thinking, *There will always be people who are not going to like me or who are disappointed in me, perhaps for many different reasons.* Suddenly interrupting my normal thought process, the Lord responded, *Yes, but I'm not one of them!* How wonderful! When we profoundly know how He feels about us, the opinions of other people really don't matter. I can always count on God's love to support me, and I can continue to grow in an ever-deepening knowledge of His great consistent affection for me.

My John Deere Experience

As I climbed into bed one evening, I felt guilty for not reading the Bible and praying that day. As I lay alone in the darkness, I decided to compensate by quoting a Bible passage until I fell asleep. I began quoting, "I have been crucified with Christ; it is no longer I who live, but Christ lives in me; and the life which I now live in the flesh I live by faith in the Son of God, who loved me and gave Himself for me" (Gal. 2:20).

As I recited this passage aloud, I so felt His presence that I decided to do it again, this time slowly, speaking the verse phrase by phrase. As I meditated on the verse, I realized the apostle Paul was, in fact, preaching to himself. Even though he penned this letter to the Galatians, he described the Lord's love in explicitly personal terms: "who loved me and gave Himself for me." In other words, he didn't write "who loved *you Galatians*," or even "who loved *us*," but instead "who loved me"!

I decided to quote it aloud once more. As I spoke this part, *"who loved me and gave Himself for me,"* a vision of a massive green-and-yellow striped tent appeared in the spirit above me. I recognized the green and yellow as the two signature colors of the John Deere tractor company. If you have ever seen their equipment, you know the exact colors I refer to. It was as though a circus-size John Deere tent over-shadowed me. Then it disappeared as suddenly as it had appeared.

I decided to quote the verse one more time. The very same green-and-yellow tent appeared above me when I said, "Who loved me and gave Himself for me." As I pondered the meaning of the remarkable vision, I fell asleep.

When I awoke the next morning, I had completely forgotten the experience. As I drove to work, the Lord interrupted my thoughts with, *What did you think about what happened to you last night?*

Then I remembered, *Oh, yes! What was that? I didn't have a clue!*

The Lord said, *Tell me what happened.* I rehearsed the episode to Him point by point saying, "And then when I got to the part where Paul wrote of You—*who loved me and gave Himself for me*—this massive green-and-yellow John Deere–looking tent appeared over my head!"

The Lord responded tenderly, *Yes, John's dear to Me.* And that was all He said. End of conversation. Instantly I knew what He meant. He was referring to the apostle John and how well he knew that Jesus loved him. John referred to himself uniquely as "the disciple whom Jesus loved" (John 21:20). This descriptive phrase occurs four times in the Bible but only in John's gospel. None of the other apostles referred to John that way, but John knew it was true and identified himself that way in his letter.

The Lord used a play on words and the experience of being over-shadowed with the John Deere tent to communicate His love that covers my life. The John Deere (or "John's dear to the Lord") tent, appearing over me when I quoted Galatians 2:20, was a prophetic picture confirming the same truth in my life. I, too, am a disciple whom Jesus loves, but I'm not unique in that regard. He loves you in the very same way.

THE JOHN MCMILLAN AIRPLANE TICKET

I once dreamed I was at the airport about to catch an international flight. While I was at the security checkpoint, I realized the name on my ticket was John McMillan. I panicked, knowing it is virtually impossible to get through security when your ticket and ID do not match. I had no trouble passing security or boarding the flight, although my driver's license showed my name, Robert A. McMillan.

Through the dream the Lord again showed His heart toward me. My natural identity is Robert A. McMillan, or Robin, as most people know me. The identity we have from our parents or one imposed upon us by society or culture is often inaccurate. It is God who establishes and reveals to us our true ID. Once again God identified me as John, the disciple whom He loves. Moreover, He wanted me to identify myself the same way.

My Functional Identity

The Lord has given me a number of prophetic words and experiences over my lifetime that helped me recognize my functional identity. He once told me that I was a *raconteur*, a word that originates from Old French meaning "to tell." Dictionary.com defines it as "a person who is skilled in relating stories and anecdotes interestingly." That's fascinating since I often tell stories when I speak to illustrate my message. I even wrote a book titled *Mystic Moose Tales: Redefining Wildlife*, telling real-life stories written in allegorical form. My intention is to impart a love for the kind of supernatural life each of us as believers can experience. I am a raconteur!

On another occasion the Lord told me that I was a *harbinger*. A harbinger is a herald, *one that presages or foreshadows something to come*. A robin is a harbinger of springtime. When those birds show up you know springtime is just around the corner.

I come from a family full of Roberts, at least six in my immediate group of fathers, grandfathers, uncles, and cousins. My parents named me Robert, but with so many Roberts already, they always called me Robin! One aspect of my ministry involves bringing hope to those who listen. When people believe the things I tell them from the Lord, a spiritual springtime always follows. I know my true identity. I am a harbinger.

JOYFUL PHILIP

The most powerful revelation of my functional identity came in a dream more than twenty years ago. In the dream I stood in my pastor's living room when three small angels, who resembled Down Syndrome children, came in. The love of God flowed to me from them in a most amazing way.

As I picked one up she asked, "What is your name?"

I said, "Robin McMillan," and she responded, "Oh, you're Joyful Philip!"

I was taken aback by her response, wondering what she meant. Then another one of the messengers looked up at me and asked my name too. I answered and he also responded, "Oh, you're Joyful Philip." Through these small unusual messengers the Lord revealed something about my identity I had not yet fully grasped.

The one I held spoke to me again, "You *know* there is a prophetic mantle or tabernacle held up by nine pins called the 'dones of God,' don't you?"

Once again I was startled by her proclamation.

She continued, "When a man learns how to live in that place, all the fullness of God is at his disposal."

I was dumbfounded. I did not understand at all. The picture she described was of a tabernacle or tent held up by *nine pins*, a biblical word for tent posts. She said the nine posts were named the *dones* of God, but what was she talking about? I soon realized the angel had pluralized *done* to *dones*, because there were nine of them!

As I asked the Lord about the meaning of the tabernacle tent supported by nine posts (pins), or the *dones* of God, I remembered that the work of the cross was a finished work. In other words, it was *done*. One of the last things Jesus cried on the cross before His death was, "It is finished." When you study closely different aspects of the gospel message, many of the promised blessings are given in past tense. The gospel is not so much about what we must do but about believing in what Jesus has already done for us.

We find many past tense aspects of our redemption in the book of Ephesians: God "has blessed us with every spiritual blessing in the heavenly places in Christ" (Eph. 1:3); "He made us accepted" (1:6); as believers "we have redemption" (1:7); "we have obtained an inheritance" (1:11); He made you "alive" (2:1); and He "raised us up" and "made us sit together in the heavenly places" (2:6).

We discover that He "has delivered us from the power of darkness and conveyed us into the kingdom of the Son of His love" (Col. 1:13), and by His "stripes you were healed" (1 Peter 2:24).

And on it goes. If we can hear it, everything we shall accomplish in the gospel has already been accomplished for us, because "we are His workmanship, created in Christ Jesus for good works, which God prepared beforehand that we should walk in them" (Eph. 2:10).

In other words the truth of the gospel is about entering into the benefits of things that have been done for us in Christ. It truly is finished! The Nine Dones Tabernacle is a picture of what is available for us in Christ. It speaks of a place we can live where we enjoy and learn to live in all the fullness of God now available to us. Paul prayed for us "to know the love of Christ which passes knowledge; that you may be filled with all the fullness of God" (Eph. 3:19). We may be filled with all the fullness of God by knowing His love. That is a promise almost too amazing to believe.

A TABERNACLE OF SAFETY

In these two separate encounters the Lord used a tent or tabernacle as prophetic pictures. They represent two aspects of God, His love and what He accomplished for us in Christ. The John Deere tent speaks of His love for us. The Nine Dones Tabernacle speaks of the many aspects of what He provided for us in the finished work of Christ. In Isaiah God promised He will provide for us a unique place of safety: "There will be a tabernacle for shade in the daytime from the heat, for a place of refuge, and for a shelter from storm and rain" (Isa. 4:6). David called it the "secret place of the Most High" (Ps. 91:1), a place of safety, security, and provision.

I began to understand why the messengers called me Joyful Philip. Philip was a New Testament evangelist who preached Christ in the city of Samaria. As the people believed his message, they heard and saw great miracles, "and there was great joy in that city" (Acts 8:8).

Several years after I had this dream, manifestations of laughter and spiritual drunkenness occurred in certain branches of the church. In Rodney Howard Browne's meetings and the Toronto Outpouring, characterized by the Father's love, laughter became a well-publicized phenomenon. In my own meetings as well, joy and laughter became normal responses many times as I spoke. Just as the ministry of Philip the evangelist resulted in great joy, I, too, saw joy released in my ministry. I realize that Joyful Philip is a part of my functional identity.

Who Are You?

God wants each of us to know who He created us to be and what He's created us to do. An experiential knowledge of His love is vital to realizing both. Deliverance from criticism and the critical spirit, found on the second wagon in my vision, removes two huge obstacles from our path.

Eight

ENEMY OF HOPE

Another aspect of criticism distorts who God created us to be. It's our criticism of others. And just as we need deliverance from negative words spoken over our own lives, we must be set free from our propensity to criticize and judge others. This criticism is pride based, and since "God resists the proud, but gives grace to the humble" (James 4:6), it restricts the flow of God's grace that enables us to discover and enjoy who He created us to be.

CYNICISM: FALSE WISDOM

Criticism and cynicism are evil twins. Many regard cynicism as though it were a virtue, when in fact it is a powerful deception, often embraced as an emotional anesthetic for hurts and wounds. At first it deadens the pain of rejection and disappointment, but ultimately it numbs us to the mercy of God that heals us. Cynicism is like a negative lens through which we see the world. It disguises itself as a counterfeit wisdom, posing as an expert, finding fault with things and people. Anyone can criticize, but where is that person who looks at imperfect people and negative situations and brings redemptive solutions? That's what true wisdom does. It builds; it comforts; it encourages. It may correct, but it's always redemptive.

The psalmist identified an unlimited realm of fruitfulness available to those who refuse to be critical:

> Blessed is the man
> Who walks not in the counsel of the ungodly,
>> Nor stands in the path of sinners,
>> Nor sits in the seat of the scornful;
> But his delight is in the law of the LORD,
>> And in His law he meditates day and night.
> He shall be like a tree
>> Planted by the rivers of water,
>> That brings forth its fruit in its season,
>> Whose leaf also shall not wither;
> And whatever he does shall prosper.
>
> (Ps. 1:1–3)

The blessed do not sit in the seat of the scornful. They do not *position* themselves to scoff, to criticize, or be derisive. Instead, they delight in the ways of the Lord, which are redemptive, consistently fruitful, and enable them to prosper. Christ Jesus fully embodied this attitude when He said, "If anyone hears My words and does not believe, I do not judge him; for I did not come to judge the world but to save the world" (John 12:47).

THE HAMAN PRINCIPLE

Our unrighteous judgments can determine our future troubles. The principle of reaping and sowing works in both positive and negative ways. We *will* reap what we sow, either in a way that blesses us or harms us. This truth is clearly portrayed in the book of Esther through the life of a man named Haman. His hate-filled criticism of a man named Mordecai cost him his life.

Esther is one of the most remarkable books in Scripture. Some, such as Martin Luther, have questioned its divine inspiration because God's name is never mentioned. Yet in its pages is a clear imprint of a neglected aspect of God's nature that we would be wise to embrace.

The book of Esther begins with Ahasuerus, the Medo-Persian king, searching for a wife to replace the contentious Queen Vashti. He chose a beautiful young lady named Esther, who concealed her Jewish heritage from the king. She was an orphan adopted by her cousin Mordecai, a prominent member of the court who sat at the gate, a place of authority. After Esther entered the palace, Mordecai paced daily in front of the court to learn of her welfare. While there he learned of a plot by two royal officials to murder the king. Mordecai reported the plot to Queen Esther and saved the king's life. No one informed Ahasuerus of Mordecai's loyal service, but it was recorded in the official history of the nation.

Mordecai soon encountered Haman, another member of the king's court who was a powerful and arrogant man. Mordecai, a godly man, refused to violate his conscience by bowing to acknowledge Haman's position of authority. This deeply offended Haman, whose wounded pride fed a growing hatred of Mordecai. He conspired to kill not only Mordecai, but all Jewish people as well.

At an opportune moment Haman introduced his conspiracy to the king. He said, "There is a certain people scattered and dispersed among the people in all the provinces of your kingdom; their laws are different from all other people's, and they do not keep the king's laws. Therefore it is not fitting for the king to let them remain" (Est. 3:8).

Haman convinced King Ahasuerus to legalize the annihilation of all Jewish people. He reveled in his position of favor with the king, continually boasting to his wife and friends of the glory of his riches and prominence in the court. But even with such abundant honor, he seethed whenever he saw Mordecai sitting at the king's gate, refusing to pay him homage.

His wife and friends advised Haman to construct a seventy-five-foot gallows and use it to publicly hang his despised enemy, Mordecai. The night before the planned execution, the king could not sleep. He called for the historic record, where he discovered that Mordecai had once saved his life. King Ahasuerus determined then to honor Mordecai for his courage.

The next morning Haman entered the king's court with the express purpose of gaining the king's permission to hang Mordecai. Before he made his request the king asked him what he would do to honor a great man. Haman assumed he himself was the great man the king wanted to honor and thus replied, "Let a royal robe be brought which the king has worn, and a horse on which the king has ridden, which has a royal crest placed on its head. Then let this robe and horse be delivered to the hand of one of the king's most noble princes, that he may array the man. . . . Then parade him on horseback through the city" (Est. 6:8–9).

The king liked Haman's idea so much that he ordered Haman to do that very thing—for Mordecai: "Hurry, take the robe and the horse, as you have suggested, and do so for Mordecai the Jew who sits within the king's gate. Leave nothing undone of all that you have spoken" (Est. 6:10).

Haman returned home completely mortified. The tables were now turning. Everyone realized that the evil he intended for Mordecai would return upon his own head. Mordecai's favor and Haman's profound wickedness suddenly endangered his own life. Then the royal court summoned Haman to a banquet sponsored by Queen Esther. Her hidden purpose for the banquet was to reveal Haman's plan to destroy Mordecai and all the Jews.

Haman arrived at the feast Esther prepared for him and the king. On the second day King Ahasuerus declared to Esther:

> "What is your petition, Queen Esther? It shall be granted you. And what is your request, up to half the kingdom? It shall be done!"
>
> Then Queen Esther answered and said, "If I have found favor in your sight, O king, and if it pleases the king, let my life be given me at my petition, and my people at my request. For we have been sold, my people and I, to be destroyed, to be killed, and to be annihilated. Had we been sold as male and female slaves, I would have held my tongue, although the enemy could never compensate for the king's loss."
>
> So King Ahasuerus answered and said to Queen Esther, "Who is he, and where is he, who would dare presume in his heart to do such a thing?"
>
> And Esther said, "The adversary and enemy is this wicked Haman!"
>
> So Haman was terrified before the king and queen. (Est. 7:2–6)

Haman's plot enraged the king when he realized it endangered the life of his beloved Queen Esther. A close confidant then informed him of the gallows Haman built for Mordecai's death. King Ahasuerus commanded that Haman be executed on it: "So they hanged Haman on the gallows that he had prepared for Mordecai" (Est. 7:10).

How sobering! Haman died because he allowed a critical spirit to rule his life. He died on the very gallows he'd built to execute Mordecai.

Learning My Lessons

I worked almost twenty years in the food service equipment indus-
try. I earned my living by selling commercial cooking equipment and
supplies. If I sold it, installed it, and collected for it, I received a per-
centage of the sales for my pay. Eventually I made an excellent salary
that doubled each year for a while.

Our company employed an installation crew, who were paid
hourly wages to deliver, uncrate, and set in place—according to the
blueprints of each job—the equipment I sold. One crew member
became jealous of the amount of money I earned. It was common for
me to find his extinguished cigarettes in my desk drawer. While I was
calling on customers, he often ate his lunch at my desk. It was not unusual for me to find parts of his ham sandwich or other food particles
on my desk or even on my telephone. Of course, he never admitted to
the infractions, but it didn't take a private detective to determine who
continued sabotaging my office space. I fumed for weeks, determining
to get even. One day my opportunity came. (Picture me here smiling
with evil glee!)

I discovered the "person of interest" outside in the parking lot
washing the company installation truck. I perched myself on the load-
ing dock that stood three feet above him in a strategic location. I stood
there in my suit and tie watching him for a moment wet and soap up
the truck. Then I noticed his live water hose lying at my feet.

I thought, *Now is the time to get even with him. I'll pick up the
hose and wet this wicked perpetrator but good.* In a few minutes I had
an important appointment with a customer across town, and I knew I
needed to act quickly. I picked up the water hose by its pistol-grip spray
nozzle, zeroed in on his rotund, jealous carcass, and aimed it squarely
at his broad back. As I began to squeeze the handle, I relented and

turned the spray nozzle just to the left of him so he wouldn't actually get wet. I just wanted to let him know I could get him if I wanted to—not considering that the Lord could get me anytime *He* wanted to. I didn't realize I picked up the pistol grip spray nozzle backward. When I squeezed the handle the water shot back at me, right beside my ear. Had I decided to soak him I would have completely soaked myself—suit, shirt, tie, and all! I would have received the exact measure of punishment I had chosen for him. Actually, I did receive it. Since I had mercy on him, I had mercy on myself, and I determined the measure.

A continual pattern of failure and distress often indicates that we are guilty of unrighteous judgments toward others. God will deliver us from these patterns of criticism and judgment as we humble ourselves before Him.

Have you been constructing your own gallows? If so, tear them down now. Jesus instructed us to live in a much higher way when He said, "I say to you, love your enemies, bless those who curse you, do good to those who hate you, and pray for those who spitefully use you and persecute you, that you may be sons of your Father in heaven; for He makes His sun rise on the evil and on the good, and sends rain on the just and on the unjust" (Matt. 5:44–45).

The prophet Hosea observed, "Thus judgment springs up like hemlock in the furrows of the field" (Hos. 10:4). In the ancient world, people took hemlock to commit suicide. Our unrighteous judgment of others is like spiritual suicide, killing *us*, as the Lord Jesus Himself made so clear when He taught, "Judge not, that you be not judged. For with what judgment you judge, you will be judged; and with the measure you use, it will be measured back to you" (Matt. 7:1–2). That cycle of criticism must be broken.

We will reap what we sow. If we expect to reap mercy, we must sow mercy every opportunity we get. If we bless others, we will be blessed. We must "be kindly affectionate to one another with brotherly love, in honor giving preference to one another" (Rom. 12:10). Instead of sowing the wind and reaping a whirlwind (Hos. 8:7), we who truly "sow to the Spirit will of the Spirit reap everlasting life" (Gal. 6:8). As we adopt the remedy of sowing to the Spirit, of honoring all men, we will find our lives changing and our true identities emerging. God will deliver us from criticism and the critical spirit if we will just let Him.

Part Four

WAGON THREE:
ABUNDANT HOPE

Nine

PRISONERS OF HOPE

The third wagon I saw in my encounter overflowed with the abundant hope God provides through the gospel. Many people, discouraged and blinded by difficult circumstances, have become prisoners of depression and unbelief. As Zechariah warned, we must "return to the stronghold, you prisoners of hope. Even today I declare that I will restore double to you" (Zech. 9:12). We must return to the stronghold of God's nature revealed in the redemptive stories of how He dealt with mankind down through the ages. Through those biblical testimonies and inspired by hope, we can exercise our faith to obtain all God has promised us. The gospel has the potential to restore a double blessing for all our losses and to make us completely different kinds of prisoners—*prisoners of hope!*

OUR DYSFUNCTIONAL FOREFATHERS

To appreciate God's perfect nature we must consider our spiritual fore-fathers and other great heroes of the faith in the context of how God helped and used them. Abraham, Isaac, and Jacob are the patriarchs of our faith and yet leaders of a morally flawed and dysfunctional family. To save their own skins, Abraham and Isaac both lied about their wives being their sisters. Their children schemed, lied, and betrayed one another. Exacting revenge for raping their sister, Jacob's sons murdered all the men in one city and then plundered their goods and enslaved their women and children (Gen. 34). The many tales of these patriarchs' failures and wicked indiscretions are staggering. Why on earth would God choose such men to spearhead our faith and establish His household?

And consider these heroes of our faith, many in the lineage of the Messiah: Adam and Eve disobeyed God's only command and through their rebellion unleashed corruption upon the entire human race. Noah got drunk and pronounced a curse upon one of his sons. Moses murdered an Egyptian taskmaster. Elijah suffered from depression and fled in panic and abject cowardice from a woman. Sarah, the wife of Abraham, forced her servant girl and child into the desert to die. Jacob was a con man who outfoxed his brother in a time of weakness, taking his birthright and then defrauding him of his blessing.

Jacob's family was a disaster on several counts. His sons sold their brother Joseph into slavery and lied to their father about Joseph's death. Joseph was proud, bragged about his calling, and incurred his brothers' wrath. Gideon was fearful, Samson had a lust problem, and Rahab was a prostitute. Samuel had rebellious and ungodly children. David was an adulterer and murderer. The Samaritan woman at the well had five husbands, and Mary Magdalene had seven demons. Peter denied the Lord with oaths and curses, and all the apostles deserted Jesus when He needed them the most. The great apostle Paul had once consented to Stephen's murder and persecuted and imprisoned the church Jesus died to save.

Couldn't God have chosen a more righteous family than Abraham and his offspring? Were there not more deserving and exemplary people available? God's wisdom cannot be denied. He revealed His heart toward these three men, continually identifying Himself as the God of Abraham, the God of Isaac, and the God of Jacob, claiming them as His own. It seems like God found in them a highly dysfunctional family to use as a prototype for the people of God. Why? I believe it was to reveal His nature, to demonstrate His power to redeem and transform, and to release hope to the world.

Isaiah's prophecy revealed that God chose the poor, the brokenhearted, the imprisoned, and the depressed to become trees of righteousness (Isa. 61:1–3). God empowered these tragically fallen people to show the world what He could do with such men and women. From them God would produce a lineage that would become a kingdom of royal priests. This spiritual nobility would one day govern the world in a righteous and honorable way. The apostle Peter described them this way: "You are a chosen generation, a royal priesthood, a holy nation, His own special people, that you may proclaim the praises of Him who called you out of darkness into His marvelous light; who once were not a people but are now the people of God, who had not obtained mercy but now have obtained mercy" (1 Peter 2:9–10).

We must acknowledge that our God truly is the God of hope—hope built on God's proven nature and His abundant promises. As we read the life stories of our spiritual forefathers, full of failure and destruction, we see God's repeated redemptive interventions. If God picked them we can be sure He won't reject us as we come to Him in humility and faith. We find hope for our own lives and families because we know who He is and what He is like. He is never surprised by anything we do, never left without an answer for any generation, any problem, or the challenges facing any culture. Remember, before mankind ever needed a Savior, God provided one. Christ is "the Lamb slain from the foundation of the world" (Rev. 13:8). He knows the end before the beginning and had the solution before we had a problem. He always does.

CYRUS

Our ability to hope, then, is fueled by the historic evidence of God's care for His people and His foreknowledge of human history. He provides solutions for difficult situations before they exist. The storied lives of Cyrus, king of Persia and conqueror of the Babylonian Empire, and Josiah, king of Judah, are two such examples.

Almost two hundred years before the Jews were exiled to Babylon and Solomon's temple was destroyed, Isaiah prophesied of King Cyrus who would restore both Jerusalem and the temple:

> Who confirms the word of His servant,
> And performs the counsel of His messengers;
> Who says to Jerusalem, "You shall be inhabited,"
> To the cities of Judah, "You shall be built,"
> And I will raise up her waste places;
> Who says to the deep, "Be dry!
> And I will dry up your rivers";
> Who says of *Cyrus*, "He is My shepherd,
> And he shall perform all My pleasure,"
> Saying to Jerusalem, "You shall be built,"
> And to the temple, "Your foundation shall be laid."
>
> (ISA. 44:26–28)

Between 606 BC and 588 BC, Nebuchadnezzar, king of Babylon, invaded the Jewish nation and deported its people to Babylon in three different waves. The temple was destroyed and remained in decay for seventy years. Years later the Persian Empire conquered Babylon, and a man named Cyrus became their king. In the first year of his reign, he enabled the Jewish exiles to return to Jerusalem and ordered work to begin to restore the temple at his own expense. According to the Jewish historian Josephus, Cyrus initiated this restoration because he read of himself in Isaiah's prophecy, written 150–200 years before he was born.

JOSIAH

In the same prophetic spirit as Isaiah, an unnamed Jewish prophet made a similar decree:

> And behold, a man of God went from Judah to Bethel by the word of the LORD, and Jeroboam stood by the altar to burn incense. Then he cried out against the altar by the word of the LORD, and said, "O altar, altar! Thus says the LORD: 'Behold, a child, *Josiah* by name, shall be born to the house of David; and on you he shall sacrifice the priests of the high places who burn incense on you, and men's bones shall be burned on you.'" And he gave a sign the same day, saying, "This is the sign which the LORD has spoken: Surely the altar shall split apart, and the ashes on it shall be poured out."
>
> So it came to pass when King Jeroboam heard the saying of the man of God, who cried out against the altar in Bethel, that he stretched out his hand from the altar, saying, "Arrest him!" Then his hand, which he stretched out toward him, withered, so that he

could not pull it back to himself. The altar also was split apart, and the ashes poured out from the altar, according to the sign which the man of God had given by the word of the LORD. (1 Kings 13:1–5)

The prophet identified Josiah by name 360 years before Josiah was born. Josiah instituted a spiritual renewal in Israel that reversed the nation's terrible fall into idolatry. Josiah turned the nation back to God, and just as the man of God decreed, he burned the bones of the false prophets upon that very altar. "The three decades of Josiah's reign were characterized by peace, prosperity, and reform. Hence, they were among the happiest years experienced by Judah. King Josiah devoted himself to pleasing God and reinstituting Israel's observance of the Mosaic Law."[1]

God made provision more than three hundred years in advance of Israel's need. Israel's history testifies once again to the delivering power of the God of hope.

HOPE OF THE FOUR LEPERS

Four lepers demonstrated remarkable hope in the midst of a terrible famine. In the days of Elisha, Ben Hadad gathered his Syrian army and laid siege to Samaria, causing great distress to the king of Israel. Food was scarce and valuable. People ate everything imaginable and some things that one could scarcely imagine. According to the standard of today's economy, a donkey's head sold for six hundred dollars, and a cup of dove's dung cost forty. Some desperate, starving people committed the unspeakable and boiled and ate their babies.

The king of Israel blamed Elisha for the dreadful situation and sent officers to kill him. Elisha barricaded himself in his house, sought the Lord, and heard from heaven. He prophesied:

Hear the word of the LORD. Thus says the LORD: "Tomorrow about this time a seah [basket] of fine flour shall be sold for a shekel, and two seahs of barley for a shekel, at the gate of Samaria." So an officer on whose hand the king leaned answered the man of God and said, "Look, if the LORD would make windows in heaven, could this thing be?" And he said, "In fact, you shall see it with your eyes, but you shall not eat of it." (2 Kings 7:1–2)

Meanwhile four lepers sat outside the city gate. In a time of famine who could be more hopeless than lepers perched between a city with no food and an enemy army prepared to kill everyone in the vicinity? If they sat where they were, they would certainly die, and to surrender to the Syrians meant instant death. The four lepers carefully weighed their options. One said, "If we say, 'We will enter the city,' the famine is in the city, and we shall die there. And if we sit here, we die also. Now therefore, come, let us surrender to the army of the Syrians. If they keep us alive, we shall live; and if they kill us, we shall only die" (2 Kings 7:4).

Their conclusion: *"Why are we sitting here until we die?"* (2 Kings 7:3). They stood up, shook off their fear, and proceeded to the Syrian army camp. Hope offered one lone alternative if the lepers were to survive. They arose in faith and ventured forward.

When they arrived at the Syrian camp they discovered lights on but nobody home! The night before, the entire Syrian army heard a loud noise sounding like the horses and chariots of another army. The Syrians believed the king of Israel hired Hittite and Egyptian forces to attack them and fled, leaving behind absolutely everything they owned. The starving lepers ate their fill, loaded up all the silver and gold they could carry, and left to hide their treasure. They returned to the camp once more, loaded up as much booty as they could, and hid it too.

After their miraculous deliverance, a deep sense of remorse fell upon the lepers. They said to one another, "We are not doing right. This day is a day of good news, and we remain silent. If we wait until morning light, some punishment will come upon us. Now therefore, come, let us go and tell the king's household" (2 Kings 7:9).

The lepers returned to the city and with great difficulty convinced the king of Israel that the Syrians fled, leaving bountiful food and wealth. It was a day of good news. What compelled the lepers to venture to the camp of the Syrian army when no one else would? *Hope.* Hope convinced them to risk a violent death at the hands of the invaders for the chance of gaining life-saving provision.

Impoverished and despised men discovered in a moment of time the abundant availability of everything they needed. The lepers described their great deliverance as "good news," literally meaning to gladden with good news. It is no stretch for me to believe that Jesus had this story in mind when He used the word *gospel* also meaning "good news." He called His basic message "the gospel of the kingdom" of heaven.

This story is such a great picture of the hope imbedded in Jesus' message. While fear of an enemy force held an entire kingdom hostage, four lepers discovered that victory was already theirs. They simply needed to walk over and claim it. The king of Israel and the inhabitants of the city under siege were similar to many believers today. God has granted us the victory over our enemies. It is a finished work, and yet many perish from fear of a foe that has already been supernaturally defeated.

The way Jesus lived demonstrated and imparted hope in so many ways. He not only walked on water, but He inspired Peter to do it too. He had a creative answer for every situation He faced. Peter once asked Him if they should pay the temple tax the Pharisees required.

Jesus' solution was for Peter to go fishing, take the first fish off his hook, open its mouth, and pay the tax with the money he found there (Matt. 17:27).

Jesus healed every sick person who came to Him, slept through storms at sea, rebuked the winds and the waves to bring peace, and walked through the midst of angry mobs resolved to kill Him. No problem was insurmountable to Jesus. It shouldn't be to us either.

GIDEON AND THE ANGEL

In the book of Judges a frightened man named Gideon labored under the oppressive regime of the Midianites who regularly invaded Israel, stealing their weapons, their farming implements, and their harvests. He didn't know God destined him to deliver the entire nation from this oppressor. The angel of the Lord appeared to Gideon while he was threshing wheat in a winepress, hiding his small harvest from his enemies. When Gideon first saw the angel, the heavenly messenger sat calmly under a terebinth tree undismayed by the tumultuous circumstances that so afflicted the children of God. And then the angel spoke:

> "The LORD is with you, you mighty man of valor!"
>
> Gideon said to Him, "O my lord, if the LORD is with us, why then has all this happened to us? And where are all His miracles which our fathers told us about, saying, 'Did not the LORD bring us up from Egypt?' But now the LORD has forsaken us and delivered us into the hands of the Midianites."
>
> Then the LORD turned to him and said, "Go in this might of yours, and you shall save Israel from the hand of the Midianites. Have I not sent you?" (Judges 6:12–14)

The calm manner emanating from the angel demonstrated heaven's disposition of peace in the face of Gideon's turmoil, and it hinted at the level of confidence God would soon impart to His servant. His words so surprised the fearful Gideon: "The LORD is with you, you mighty man of valor!" A mighty man of valor? That description was the opposite of Gideon's experience and his present circumstances. He threshed wheat in an enclosed winepress rather than in the open threshing floor in fear of the marauding Midianites.

The angel did not describe Gideon's present condition. He was re-creating him by imparting to him a transforming grace if he would but hear and believe. The angel's words alone contained sufficient power to impart hope and transform troubled Gideon. Why did the angel tell Gideon that the Lord was with him? No outward evidence proved it. The messenger of God arrived to expose Gideon to a higher reality he did not yet comprehend.

God *was* with him. He simply needed a renewed mind, one that believed what the Lord could do through him. The same God is with us too. God's Word contains the power to conquer our circumstances by transforming us and changing our perception of reality. Angels are messengers of hope. "Are not they all ministering spirits to render service, sent on a commission for the sake of those who are about to inherit salvation?" (Heb. 1:14 WET). They give us heaven's perspective and always impart hope. They enable us to apprehend the kind of salvation that empowers us to overcome any circumstance.

AN ENCOURAGING HOPE ENCOUNTER

I awakened one morning in the midst of a spiritual encounter, looking directly into the cheerful smiling face of a man named Charles Hope.

He wore a hat and sweatshirt, both inscribed with the logo of the Philadelphia Eagles football team. Hope smiled at me broadly and exuberantly exclaimed, "Hello, I'm going to be your new best friend." In my encounter the Lord revealed to me that this man was a rogue.

This strange encounter emphasized the reality of true biblical hope. There is profound spiritual revelation in the name Charles Hope. *Charles* means "free man" or "warrior." The Lord described him as a "rogue," meaning "one who operates outside normal or desirable controls; one who is mischievous; a playful person." I thought of descriptions I have read of rogue elephants. No one could control them. Where does a rogue elephant sit? Anywhere he wants to! He *is* uncontrollable.

The hope we have is rogue-like. It is so free that no man or circumstance can control it. It exists for us outside the normal pressures, principles, and patterns of our time/space world. That man of hope was a type of our Lord Jesus, the true free man of hope. Our heavenly hope is an ultimate depository of functional freedom found in the Man death could not contain. To be filled with that hope makes us spiritual warriors that cannot be defeated.

THE PHILADELPHIA EAGLE CONNECTION

Previously, when I encountered the five wagons, I found myself in a heavenly place under the wing of the great eagle described in Psalm 91. And now this man named Hope was marked with an eagle, the logo of Philadelphia Eagles National Football League team. It is a prophetic picture of the great eagle and our access to the heavens that ensures us a constant enjoyment of true biblical hope.

The Philadelphia Eagles logo on the hat and the sweatshirt speaks of the power of a loving community, the importance of learning how to live in the Spirit, and the redemptive heart of God. The eagle logo stamped on the hat covering his head and sweatshirt covering his chest signified how hope covers and protects both our hearts and minds. The word *Philadelphia*, the name of the church identified in Revelation 3, means "brotherly love" and refers to the love Christians have for each other as fellow members of a loving, honoring, relational community. The church at Philadelphia was one of the two churches Jesus did not rebuke in the book of Revelation. It is in that kind of loving community where the atmosphere of hope is most readily obtained, cultivated, manifested, and enjoyed.

HOPE IS REDEMPTIVE

The Lord used the picture of the Philadelphia Eagles to speak of the redemptive heart of God through the actions of Andy Reid, a former NFL coach of the Eagles. Coach Reid gave Michael Vick a chance to play again after his humiliating imprisonment for involvement in the illegal practice of dog fighting. Reid identified qualities in Michael Vick others were unable or unwilling to see and restored his hope in a most exemplary and remarkable way.

HOPE: THE INCUBATOR OF GREAT FAITH

The writer of the book of Hebrews concluded that faith is the substance of our hope. He said, "Now faith is the substance of things hoped for, the evidence of things not seen" (Heb. 11:1). Faith is our ability to *realize* in our experience the things we hope for. You might say that faith gives us *real eyes* to realize and lay hold of what we are hoping for. We will never develop our faith beyond our ability to have the true biblical kind of hope, the confident expectation of good that God wants us to have. The person with the most hope always prevails. Hope is essential for experiencing revival in our nation, for changing our culture, and for the transformation of our society.

True hope does not disappoint because the love of God poured out in our hearts enables us to sustain our faith until His promise is fulfilled. Paul said it this way, "Now hope does not disappoint, because the love of God has been poured out in our hearts by the Holy Spirit who was given to us" (Rom. 5:5). We must remember the father of our faith, Abraham. Like father, like son, we must maintain our hope until the fulfillment of the promise, no matter how impossible it may look, feel, seem, or be. For Abraham "being beyond hope, upon the basis of hope believed, in order that he might become father of many nations, according to that which has been spoken with finality, 'In this manner will your offspring be'" (Rom. 4:16 WET).

GRAPES AND RAISINS, PROMISES AND FULFILLMENTS

Through the years I have accumulated a number of unfulfilled personal promises from the Lord. Once in prayer I asked why I had not yet seen them fulfilled. As I questioned the Lord I saw a picture in my mind of a scoop in heaven pouring out raisins. I couldn't shake free from the vision and began to ask the Lord about it.

I then realized that grapes are a clear Old Testament prophetic image representing a promise. When the twelve spies returned from spying out the promised land, they brought back enormous grapes as a tangible promise and proof of its great fruitfulness. Those grapes of Eschol were so large that it took two men to carry back one bunch supported on a long stick between them. Grapes became synonymous with the promised land and are the prototypical picture of a promise.

Raisins are dried up grapes. They don't look nearly as good as plump juicy grapes, but they fulfill a different purpose. In the ancient world they sustained soldiers in times of war and energized people traveling distances who needed nonperishable, nutritious food. Grapes only last a short time, but raisins sustain people in dry difficult circumstances over the long haul.

The Lord showed me through my vision a vital principle: *promises come like grapes but are fulfilled like raisins.* Over time our personal promises seem to dry up, much like grapes that become raisins. These promises begin to look shriveled up, puny, and of little value. The prophet Jeremiah once said, "Your words were found, and I ate them, and Your word was to me the joy and rejoicing of my heart" (Jer. 15:16). That is what we must do to inherit the promises of God. In hope we must eat them, chew on them, meditate upon them, consume them, and make them ours. If we eat them they shall sustain us in faith until the time our fulfillment arrives. This revelation increased my hope to see all my promises fulfilled.

Brotherly Love

Living biblical hope thrives in a community of brotherly love. Like the Philadelphia Eagles hat and sweatshirt, this hope covers our hearts and minds. This rogue-like hope cannot be controlled and is unceasingly joyful and free. By waiting on the Lord and mounting and remounting again and again into the heavenly realm we can access all the provision of God. Just as the prophet said, "Those who wait on the Lord shall renew their strength; they shall mount up with wings like eagles, they shall run and not be weary, they shall walk and not faint" (Isa. 40:31).

Hope is redemptive, intimate, and provides us with a heavenly rest. The apostle Paul opened his letter to Timothy this way: "Paul, an apostle of Jesus Christ, by the commandment of God our Savior and the Lord Jesus Christ, our hope" (1 Tim. 1:1).

Hope is the confident expectation of good. Our Hope is alive, a person in whom death has no power, named Jesus Christ the Lord. Our God is the God of hope: "Now may the God of hope fill you with all joy and peace in believing, that you may abound in hope by the power of the Holy Spirit" (Rom. 15:13).

He truly is our new best Friend!

Ten

HOPELESSNESS

Hopelessness is a delusion, the consequence of an inaccurate belief system. For many in our generation it is an enormous enemy. But it is an imposter, one that is empowered by believing a lie. Jesus said, "You shall know the truth, and the truth shall make you free" (John 8:32). Truth is transformational. It has the power to make us free. Lies have an opposite, detrimental effect. How do you know that your perception of reality is inaccurate? How do you know that what you believe is not true? You are not free. It can be just that simple.

The apostle Paul identified this relationship between what you believe and how it affects you. He wrote, "Now may the God of hope fill you with all joy and peace *in believing*, that you may abound in hope by the power of the Holy Spirit" (Rom. 15:13). Accurate believing produces joy and peace and an abundance of hope. *Acknowledging* the truth is not sufficient to bring freedom; the truth you *believe* is the only truth that liberates you. In some cases you may have your facts straight but still be bound because your understanding is inaccurate. Jesus warned us to "take heed *how* you hear" (Luke 8:18). If you have drawn inaccurate conclusions, you heard wrong. Allow the Holy Spirit to interpret reality for you.

JEREMIAH'S DILEMMA

Jeremiah, one of the greatest Old Testament prophets, walked close to the Lord and was one of His spokesmen of his generation to the nation of Israel. Yet this great prophet was prone to periods of hopelessness and depression. In despair he issued his complaint against the Lord and lamented, "Why is my pain perpetual and my wound incurable, which refuses to be healed? Will You surely be to me like an unreliable stream, as waters that fail?" (Jer. 15:18).

Jeremiah accused the Lord of being unreliable "as waters that fail," meaning "waters that cannot be trusted." God's response is particularly illuminated in the Amplified Bible, Classic Edition:

> Therefore thus says the Lord [to Jeremiah]: If you return [and give up this mistaken tone of distrust and despair], then I will give you again a settled place of quiet and safety, and you will be My minister; and if you separate the precious from the vile [cleansing your own heart from unworthy and unwarranted suspicions concerning God's faithfulness], you shall be My mouthpiece. . . . For I am with you to save and deliver you, says the Lord.
>
> And I will deliver you out of the hands of the wicked, and I will redeem you out of the palms of the terrible and ruthless tyrants. (Jer. 15:19–21 AMPC)

Jeremiah was affected by a common delusion that the Lord identified as a "mistaken tone of distrust and despair." His solution was simple and profound: Give it up! Stop believing the lie, reconsider your conclusions, and change your mind.

David the psalmist declared, "I would have despaired, unless I had believed that I would see the goodness of the Lord in the land of the living" (Ps. 27:13 NASB). David knew what destroys despair: having an accurate understanding that God is good, and holding a deep conviction that he would experience that goodness while he lived. Our human tendency is to allow how we feel to affect what we believe. True humility refuses to believe what we think or feel when it contradicts the truth and the revealed nature of God. Having a renewed mind is the key that brings this breakthrough.

Circumstantial deliverance is often preceded by emotional deliverance based on changing our beliefs. Jeremiah's experiential freedom was contingent on first walking in an internal freedom. The Lord promised him a new "settled place of quiet and safety" on the other side of rejecting his mistaken tone. The term "mistaken tone" reveals how easy it is to misinterpret reality. The prophet's inaccurate thought process caused him to feel depressed, and it distorted his understanding of the nature of God. The Lord also instructed Jeremiah to cleanse himself from being suspicious of God's motives. If Jeremiah made those two internal adjustments, God promised to make him His mouthpiece and would not allow Jeremiah's ever-present enemies to prevail against him. God would deliver and redeem him.

According to Jeremiah's own words, he made a significant transition to a more accurate understanding of God's heart. The Lord Himself said to him, "I know the thoughts that I think toward you, says the LORD, thoughts of peace and not of evil, to give you a future and a hope" (Jer. 29:11). Our generation needs to make the same shift in perspective and give up our "mistaken tones of distrust and despair" and "suspicions concerning God's faithfulness." Don't let hopelessness steal your joy. Identify the lies that you believe. Replace them with the truth and send despair running for its life.

CONSIDER JESUS

Let's consider another prophet. Jesus, *the Prophet* from Nazareth was born to die a terrible death, and He knew it. He suffered on a cross to a degree that perhaps no one completely understands. He walked steadfastly toward that dreadful appointment His entire life. According to Isaiah's ancient prophecy, Jesus was "a Man of sorrows and acquainted with grief" (Isa. 53:3), yet He consistently demonstrated characteristics of a hope-filled man. Jesus lived and drew His strength from the manifest presence of God. As a result He championed, proclaimed, and demonstrated the kingdom of God, typified by righteousness, peace, and joy.

Jesus was joyful because of His closeness to the Father. Many don't see God the Father as being joyful, but men of spiritual insight, such as G. K. Chesterton, believed that God's mirth was His best kept secret! Both Old and New Testaments testify that joy was a primary characteristic of Jesus' life and ministry and His unique kind of anointing. Scripture says, "Therefore God, Your God, has anointed You with the oil of gladness more than Your companions" (Heb. 1:9).

The anointing speaks of that which empowers you to do the will of God. Jesus was acquainted with sorrow and grief but known by widespread reputation as a man of joy. Jesus was anointed with the most *essential* oil: the oil of gladness. He was so joyful, in fact, that His enemies accused Him of being a drunkard. Even when being misunderstood He responded with joy, being so captivated with the goodness of His Father and eternal realities: "In that hour Jesus rejoiced in the Spirit and said, 'I thank You, Father, Lord of heaven and earth, that You have hidden these things from the wise and prudent and revealed them to babes. Even so, Father, for so it seemed good in Your sight'" (Luke 10:21).

Jesus *rejoiced*, meaning He "jumped for joy." Do you have room for a jumping Jesus, a man so happy He bounces up and down like a rubber ball? He was a happy Man. Jesus didn't just believe the truth, He was the truth. He was not just our example but is the very life force that lives within each believer. He didn't just give us *an* antidote for hopelessness; He became *the* perfect antidote. Therefore joy and gladness should be a primary characteristic of those who embrace and walk in truth.

Just as Jesus viewed life from His Father's heart, from the realm of the kingdom of God, we, too, need to see from heaven's vantage point. As we do, true hope will arise and transform the atmosphere of our lives, our cities, our countries, and our generation. It is the restoration of this hope that I proclaim through the pages of this book. Jesus Himself is the ultimate harbinger of hope.

Eleven

HOPE RESTORED

The day men murdered Christ Jesus marked the darkest day in human history, sending shock waves throughout the cosmos. Nature convulsed as an earthquake shook the ancient city of Jerusalem. The sun hid its face for three hours after Jesus breathed His last, and supernatural darkness covered the land. Two noble and brave Pharisees, Joseph of Arimathea and Nicodemus, secured Jesus' body, bloodied and bruised beyond recognition, and they laid Him to rest in a borrowed tomb.

The disillusioned apostles scattered as their hearts broke and their minds reeled in numbing disbelief. Simon Peter denied the Lord three times, just as Jesus foretold. From their human perspective Jesus' mission had completely failed. Cleopas, a disciple of Jesus, described the despair that flooded His followers: "The chief priests and our rulers delivered Him to be condemned to death, and crucified Him. But we were hoping that it was He who was going to redeem Israel" (Luke 24:20–21).

Human hope died that dark afternoon as their crucified Master took the disciples' dreams to the grave. They didn't know that from the bowels of that tragedy God would birth a new, unquenchable hope, one fueled with resurrection life and unaffected by any evil power. Despair yielded up its once-proud sovereign rule over mankind as God reversed what looked like failure in a single flash of unparalleled power. Hope's tomb became the womb of eternal life, for in the Person of the resurrected Christ, God restored hope.

Hope is the confident expectation of good, finding its source in God. It is His fundamental state of mind; therefore, the Bible calls Him "the God of hope" (Rom. 15:13). God's hope is not like natural human hope, mere positive thinking that dissipates and disappoints. His hope is alive and unaffected by outside influence. The apostle Peter described this hope that we attain through the new-birth experience, writing that we were born into "a living hope through the resurrection of Jesus Christ from the dead" (1 Peter 1:3). Our hope is not just *like* His, it *is* His—alive in us!

The basic message of the gospel is one filled with hope, the anticipation of good things. Jesus proclaimed and demonstrated this gospel, good news or glad tidings, of the kingdom of God. At His birth the angel of the Lord spoke to the shepherds, saying, "Do not be afraid, for behold, I bring you good tidings of great joy which will be to all people" (Luke 2:10). His message to the shepherds is literally interpreted, "I evangelize unto you 'great joy which is for everybody.'"

The gospel brings such hope that our joy gets evangelized! When we believe the gospel, God imparts life-changing confidence to us known as "the hope of the gospel" (Col. 1:23). Christ Jesus is personified as "our hope" (1 Tim. 1:1) and is the "hope of glory" (Col. 1:27), who abides within each believer. God has called us to live an exceedingly hope-filled life.

HOPE REVEALED IN NEW TESTAMENT STORIES

The new covenant, a covenant of grace, when understood and embraced imparts hope to us that draws us near to God. The term *grace* had multiple meanings in the ancient world. The apostle Paul used it to mean "kindness shown without regard to the worth or merit of the one who receives it in spite of what that person deserves."[1] It is also the empowerment to live a transformed life. Simply put, grace is a pure gift, something that cannot be earned. To accurately know God is to know grace. When we encounter God's grace, hope is imparted to our hearts.

The new covenant is superior to the old, containing better promises. "Now He has obtained a more excellent ministry, inasmuch as He is also Mediator of a better covenant, which was established on better promises" (Heb. 8:6). These better promises are the source of our hope, which draws us to the Lord Himself, just as the writer of Hebrews stated, "On the one hand there is an annulling of the former commandment because of its weakness and unprofitableness, for the law made nothing perfect; on the other hand, there is the bringing in of a better hope, through which we draw near to God" (Heb. 7:18–19).

Our hope is secure because God, who cannot lie, made the very promises that produce it:

Thus God, determining to show more abundantly to the heirs of promise the immutability of His counsel, confirmed it by an oath, that by two immutable things, in which it is impossible for God to lie, we might have strong consolation, who have fled for refuge to lay hold of the hope set before us. This hope we have as an anchor of the soul, both sure and steadfast, and which enters the Presence behind the veil. (Heb. 6:17–19)

Hope securely built upon the "better promises" of God anchors our soul in the presence of God and will not disappoint us. It has fueled the fire of faith that has produced every major spiritual breakthrough down through the ages.

Hope is like a spiritual bubble or sphere. Abiding in that sphere creates attitudes of confidence. It becomes the inward spiritual environment that fortifies our patience and sustains the power of the Holy Spirit in our lives. Paul wrote, "We were saved in the sphere of hope. But hope that has been seen is not hope, for that which a person sees, why does he hope for it? But if that which we do not see, we hope for, through patience we expectantly wait for it" (Rom. 8:24–25 WET).

Because Paul lived in that hope atmosphere he boldly proclaimed, "We know that all things work together for good to those who love God, to those who are the called according to His purpose" (Rom. 8:28).

Authentic biblical hope gives us the *inner knowing* that God works everything for our good who love Him and are called in accordance with His purpose. This hope inspires faith and helps us fully complete God's plan for our lives as it draws from God those very things we are expecting.

Living in hope expresses confidence in God's goodness and becomes a self-perpetuating process that enables us to live the abundant life we all desire. Our faith will never grow beyond the level of our hope. It is the source of robust faith, for "faith is the substance of things hoped for" (Heb. 11:1).

Paul was a living example of someone who walked in hope, and he prayed for us, "Now may the God of hope fill you with all joy and peace in believing, that you may abound in hope by the power of the Holy Spirit" (Rom. 15:13). *Abound* means to have more than necessary or to have in super abundance. Hope sustains the human heart and, like a magnet attracts iron, it attracts the abundant life the Lord intends for us to have. Paul wanted the Roman believers to abound in hope, knowing it was a key to unlock the door of God's storehouse of blessing.

Hope sustained Paul even while imprisoned in the Philippian jail, inspiring him to write, "In everything give thanks; for this is the will of God in Christ Jesus for you" (1 Thess. 5:18). Hope inspired Paul and Silas to sing praises to God at midnight. No jail could hold such men in its clutches. Nature itself responded to their praises as an earthquake suddenly shook that dungeon, freeing all its prisoners. Earthshaking hope still releases prisoners from the dark, dank cells of life that hold so many captive.

HOPE REVEALED IN OLD TESTAMENT STORIES

The Old Testament is filled with stories of God's intervention in the lives of His people as an amazing and ongoing *liturgy* of hope. He convinced Noah to build a boat that saved humanity from the flood. When Sodom and Gomorrah teetered on the brink of annihilation, God sent angels to save Lot and his family from imminent destruction. In Moses' day, when an enraged Egyptian army pursued the fleeing Hebrew slave force, God rolled back the Red Sea, clearing a path for His people to safely cross, and then buried their enemy in the watery grave. And these are but a few of the testimonies of generations of God's love and care for His people. "Whatever things were written before were written for our learning, that we through the patience and comfort of the Scriptures might have hope" (Rom. 15:4).

JACOB'S STORY: HOPE RESTORED

The life of Jacob, one of our great patriarchs, is a dramatic example of God's restoration of hope. Jacob's name means "supplanter," so he was the deceiver who tricked his older brother out of his birthright and blessing. As I mentioned earlier, God identifies Himself as "the God of Abraham, the God of Isaac, and the God of *Jacob*" (Ex. 3:15), demonstrating His love for Jacob years before his nature or behavior changed. God's commitment to Jacob became the catalyst for him to become a new, overcoming man. One reason I love God is because He loved Jacob. And since He loved a man like Jacob, I am convinced He loves a man like me.

The Bible confirms that Jacob and his children were ordinary men, fraught with flaws and issues. God gave him remarkable promises that began before his birth when He said to Jacob's mother, Rebekah: "Two nations are in your womb, two peoples shall be separated from your body; one people shall be stronger than the other, and the older shall serve the younger" (Gen. 25:23).

Even though God promised Jacob that Esau would serve him, Jacob and Rebekah conspired to also steal Esau's blessing from his father, Isaac. Their successful scheme so enraged Esau that Jacob fled for his life to the house of his uncle, Laban. On the way to his house, the Lord visited Jacob in a dream, speaking to him from the top of a ladder that extended from the earth into heaven. Upon it ascended and descended the angels of God appointed to fulfill His promises to His servants. God promised to give Jacob the land he slept on, to bless his family such that they would be as numerous as the sands of the sea, and to bless the entire world through the seed He would give him.

God swore to go with him until He fulfilled all He'd promised. Shaken by this revelatory encounter, Jacob blurted, "'Surely the LORD is in this place, and I did not know it.' And he was afraid and said, 'How awesome is this place! This is none other than the house of God, and this is the gate of heaven!'" (Gen. 28:16–17). Jacob assumed from the encounter that the Lord made that particular place special.

Special it was, but the depth of revelation contained the truth that, ultimately, *believers* would become both that "house of God," and the gates through whom God would enter into places all over the earth through the coming of the Messiah and the establishment of the gospel. Jesus Christ, our own personal "Jacob's ladder," a functional ladder that lives inside us, became our way to access the heavens and all God has for us. Upon faith in Jesus we then become God's way to access and impact the world.

Fast-forward decades later to Jacob's old age. By then his remarkable encounter at Bethel was but a faded memory. The difficulties of life had demoralized the patriarch. Then life seemed so full of promise, but now Jacob endured a famine that threatened the very existence of his family. Moreover, his heart had been broken twenty-two years earlier when his favorite son, Joseph, did not return from searching for his brothers who tended their wandering herds. Upon hearing the news of Joseph's death, Jacob wept, "I shall go down into the grave to my son in mourning" (Gen. 37:35). His dysfunctional family languished, and Jacob despaired as all hope disintegrated.

On one single day Jacob's sorrow turned to joy as his despair was swallowed up in hope. He discovered that Joseph was still alive! Joseph was lord of all Egypt, and Jacob and his family now had access to more provision than they could ever use. In but a single moment of time, God restored Jacob's hope.

HOPE REVEALED IN MODERN-TIME STORIES

RONALD REAGAN

Ronald Reagan was our fortieth president and a renowned optimist. His hope-filled perspective infected the entire nation and helped pull us out of a long season of negativity, fear, and hopelessness. One of his favorite stories clearly expresses both his viewpoint and the attitude of the hope-filled person.

Ed Meese, attorney and longtime friend of Reagan, served with him in the White House. One time he was asked to relate one of President Reagan's favorite jokes. Meese told the joke this way:

The joke concerns twin boys of five or six. Worried that the boys had developed extreme personalities—one was a total pessimist, the other a total optimist—their parents took them to a psychiatrist.

First the psychiatrist treated the pessimist. Trying to brighten his outlook, the psychiatrist took him to a room piled to the ceiling with brand-new toys. But instead of yelping with delight, the little boy burst into tears. "What's the matter?" the psychiatrist asked, baffled. "Don't you want to play with any of the toys?"

"Yes," the little boy bawled, "but if I did I'd only break them."

Next the psychiatrist treated the optimist. Trying to dampen his outlook, the psychiatrist took him to a room piled to the ceiling with horse manure. But instead of wrinkling his nose in disgust, the optimist emitted just the yelp of delight the psychiatrist had been hoping to hear from his brother, the pessimist. Then he clambered to the top of the pile, dropped to his knees, and began gleefully digging out scoop after scoop with his bare hands. "What do you think you're doing?" the psychiatrist asked, just as baffled by the optimist as he had been by the pessimist. "With all this manure," the little boy replied, beaming, "there must be a pony in here somewhere!"[2]

COACH DEAN SMITH

We can also find inspiring examples of hope in contemporary history. Dean Smith coached the University of North Carolina basketball team for thirty-six years. He once owned the record for the most victories in NCAA history with 879. He was a highly innovative, strategic thinker and had a reputation for being loyal to each of his players. He continued to send regular notes of encouragement to many of them years after they played for him. His positive, hope-filled attitude permeated every aspect of his life.

Dean Smith's hope was contagious and proved to be the deciding factor in great victories on the court. March 2, 1974, his fourth-ranked Carolina Tar Heels trailed the Duke University Blue Devils by eight points with seventeen seconds left in the game. Coach Smith called time out, gathered his players around him, looked them in the eyes, and said, "We're in great shape. We've got them right where we want them. Isn't this fun!"

With that kind of confidence Coach Smith sent his players back on the court into a seemingly impossible situation. Carolina picked up two quick points when Bobby Jones hit two foul shots. They scored on a steal and scored again on a turnover of a Duke inbound pass, shortening the gap to two points. After Carolina rebounded on a missed Duke foul shot, Walter Davis hit a last second thirty-foot bank shot to tie the game, sending it into overtime. The Tar Heels claimed a 96–92 overtime victory that day. Carolina's win is regarded by many as the greatest comeback victory in college basketball history, inspired by Dean Smith's unshakable hope. Hope fuels victory in the face of overwhelming odds and is a devil-conquering force!

This is but a picture of what God wants to do for you and me.

Part Five

Wagon Four:
Unlimited Provision

Twelve

Accessing the Blessings of Heaven

Jesus turned water into wine to save a wedding, fed thousands from a few loaves and small fishes, healed multitudes of sick people, paid the temple tax from the mouth of a fish, and raised the dead. How did He do it? By accessing unlimited provision from the kingdom of heaven.

The fourth wagon in my encounter was filled with *unlimited provision* and was overflowing with God's abundance. To fulfill our calling in this generation, we must access what we need on the earth by laying hold of our provision from the heavenly realm, God's storehouse.

From Heaven to Earth: Jesus' Prayer Directive

Instructing His disciples to expect the kingdom of heaven to come to earth, Jesus prayed,

Our Father in heaven,

Hallowed be Your name.

Your kingdom come.

Your will be done

On earth as it is in heaven.

Give us this day our daily bread.

And forgive us our debts,

As we forgive our debtors.

And do not lead us into temptation,

But deliver us from the evil one.

For Yours is the kingdom and the power and the glory forever.

Amen.

(MATT. 6:9–13)

We call it the Lord's Prayer.

I grew up in a church that repeated the Lord's Prayer at the end of each public service. Hundreds of times I prayed, "Your kingdom come. Your will be done on earth as it is in heaven." Heaven never came to earth for me during those many years. Honestly, I didn't understand it was supposed to. My church's tradition meant much to me as I grew in grace. It was a safe place for me to learn of the Lord, but they, too, lacked understanding of the Lord's intention, as revealed in that prayer. Obviously, this very special prayer can be repeated without receiving the intended benefit.

Jesus demonstrated the fulfillment of that prayer by releasing healing, deliverance, wisdom, signs, wonders, and divine provision on the earth. Heaven retains all the things we need until someone on the earth places a specific faith demand upon it. This prayer urges us to do just that.

For example, the gospel of John includes the story of the marriage in Cana where Jesus manifested His glory. By producing more than a hundred gallons of the highest quality wine, He saved the celebration and spared the host much embarrassment when their wine ran out. Several times Jesus accessed food from heaven to feed a multitude of hungry people, with food left over. The Bible tells us that Jesus took five loaves and two small fish and "blessed and broke" them before they multiplied to feed more than five thousand people (Matt. 14:19). Jesus blessed and broke the bread, but He broke much more than that. He broke off the disciples' mind-set of presumed limitations, and He demonstrated the abundance available in the kingdom of God. That was the reality of His blessing. Heaven has abundant resources, so how then do we access them? And what restricts our access?

God intended every believer to access the blessings of heaven, but there are attitudes and actions that restrict us. Jealousy is one of them. It begins as a false kind of emotional comfort that feels good in a self-righteous way but quickly becomes a demonic trap that hinders the life of God from flowing through us. It can limit His provision and abort His promises in our lives. It is one of the most dangerous snares of our age.

An antidote to jealousy lies in giving honor to one another. When we honor and celebrate other people, God often releases the very same favor to us. Years ago a generous man gave me two boxes of silver and gold coins worth thousands of dollars. The two boxes were so heavy I needed a hand truck to move them. I had never met the man or publicly expressed any financial need. But his gift blessed Donna and me at a time when we really needed it.

I told a close friend about the gift and we praised God for my blessing. Rather than being jealous, my friend rejoiced with me over my favor and attracted the free flow of heaven's resources into his own life. Weeks later he also received two boxes of gold and silver coins!

If you are an artist, a musician, a songwriter, an hourly wage earner, or someone with a small income, guard your heart from jealousy and thank God for the favor others have. The writer of the book of Proverbs exhorted us to: "Keep your heart with all diligence, for out of it spring the issues of life. Put away from you a deceitful mouth, and put perverse lips far from you" (Prov. 4:23–24).

Learn to enjoy the goodness God deposits into your friends' lives. God may later give you that very same manifestation of heaven's wealth if you stand fast against the enemy's plan to use jealousy to steal your future and your favor.

The Scriptures instruct us to honor one another, including people in authority, as respect for authority is a major stabilizer in both society and the church. But it is important to honor *all* people. The apostles Paul and Peter stated this clearly in the New Testament: "Be kindly affectionate to one another with brotherly love, in honor giving preference to one another" (Rom. 12:10); and "Honor all people. Love the brotherhood. Fear God. Honor the king" (1 Peter 2:17).

Honoring one another doesn't just secure blessings for us. It encourages and inspires others to arise and lay hold of the destiny God has for them.

Years ago I designed commercial kitchens and became a food service equipment salesman. It was a particularly difficult and complex occupation but had huge potential for financial reward. As I struggled to make progress, I worked with a very successful older salesman. He was a veteran of World War II and served as a mechanic for General George Patton's tank corps. He knew the value and principle of imparting hope. At times he would cock his head to one side and, with a twinkle in his eye, say to me, "Robert, you have a bright future." I needed his kind and encouraging words. He wasn't jealous of me but saw my potential and encouraged me to keep moving forward. He taught me a lot about that business, and I eventually earned twice the income of many of my contemporaries. I would not have succeeded without the honor he gave me and the faith he had in me when I was a young, inexperienced salesman.

ICHIRO SUZUKI UNDERSTANDS HONOR

Ichiro Suzuki is a Japanese baseball player who came to the United States and played for the Seattle Mariners and the New York Yankees. In his first season he received the Rookie of the Year award, led the league in stolen bases, had the highest batting average, and won the Most Valuable Player of the Year award. If you include his hits from his years in Japanese professional baseball, he would be in third place for most hits, trailing only Ty Cobb and Pete Rose.

Ichiro is an amazing player but an even more amazing person. In 2004 he broke George Sisler's eighty-four-year-old record for most hits in a season. When Ichiro broke the record, Sisler's descendants attended the game to honor him. Ichiro returned the gesture:

In July 2009, while in St. Louis for his ninth All-Star appearance, Ichiro made a trip to Sisler's grave. He later told reporters, "There's not many chances to come to St. Louis. In 2004, it was the first time I crossed paths with him, and his family generously came all the way to Seattle. Above all, it was a chance. I wanted to do that for a grand upperclassman of the baseball world. I think it's only natural for someone to want to do that, to express my feelings in that way. I'm not sure if he's happy about it."

Ichiro, accompanied by his wife, Yumiko, and some friends, laid flowers at Sisler's grave at Des Peres Presbyterian Church Cemetery. Sisler, a Hall of Famer, died on March 26, 1973. His career was marked by a lifetime .340 batting average, and a .407 average in 1920. He was inducted into the Hall of Fame in 1939.[1]

Ichiro Suzuki understood the importance of honor. I am sure it released to him the grace to reach his high level of success. He once said of Sisler, "If there was no George Sisler to establish the record, there would have been no Ichiro to break it."[2] A gesture of honor of that magnitude is far too rare in our world today.

The first commandment with promise is based on honoring our parents: "Honor your father and your mother, as the LORD your God has commanded you, that your days may be long, and that it may be well with you in the land which the LORD your God is giving you" (Deut. 5:16).

It is especially important to honor the Lord with what He's given us. When we do, He will fill our lives with His goodness: "Honor the LORD with your possessions, and with the firstfruits of all your increase; so your barns will be filled with plenty, and your vats will overflow with new wine" (Prov. 3:9–10).

Our generosity honors the Lord and gives us access to heaven's unlimited provision. There are some in the body of Christ who question the validity of New Testament tithing, concluding it is legalism since it is a concept that appears in the Old Testament. The truth is, tithing predates the law, was established by Abraham, and Jesus Himself approved it as an essential practice (Luke 11:42).

It is true that we can't earn God's blessings by anything we do. But we can adopt attitudes and actions that will either release or restrict great provision. Consider this: How is it that those living under an old covenant with lesser promises were more generous than those who now live under a better new covenant with greater promises? Knowing the free forgiveness, the unearned love, and the wonderful mercy of God should produce in us an immediate and ongoing generosity unequaled in the Old Testament that far exceeds our giving a modest 10 percent.

In my early days as a Christian, the mishandling of funds by some ministries became a major public issue. I, too, joined in with disappointment and criticism of how certain leaders handled their ministries' finances.

As a young pastor, when I planted my first church, a fellow pastor warned me that criticism of how others use ministry funds would restrict my ability to receive legitimate offerings for my church. Many dissatisfied people in the body of Christ have restricted their ability to be blessed for just such a reason, even if they weren't pastors.

You may have given money to a ministry or church and concluded that leaders misused the money, and perhaps they did. Did you give it to them, or did you give it to the Lord? If you don't have specific authority to address the situation, then you have neither authority nor responsibility to do something about it. We can fall prey to a presumed sense of responsibility in such cases. Reevaluate the past situation and adopt the attitude that you gave the money to the Lord; then yield your sense of responsibility to Him to take care of the situation. He is well able to do so.

Jesus identified two aspects of life wherein we determine the measure we receive—one negative and one positive. When it comes to our judgments, meaning criticisms and condemnation of others, Jesus warned that we will receive the very same judgment we have rendered. He said, "Judge not, that you be not judged. For with what judgment you judge, you will be judged; and with the measure you use, it will be measured back to you" (Matt. 7:1–2). To avoid a negative outcome, we all must be just as merciful as our Father in heaven.

Jesus summed it up when He said,

> Therefore be merciful, just as your Father also is merciful. Judge not, and you shall not be judged. Condemn not, and you shall not be condemned. Forgive, and you will be forgiven. Give, and it will be given to you: good measure, pressed down, shaken together, and running over will be put into your bosom. For with the same measure that you use, it will be measured back to you. (Luke 6:36–38)

That means we will receive blessings, finances, and mercies to the degree that we have given to others. His measure in Luke's gospel is defined as "good measure, pressed down, shaken together, and running over," a phrase describing how to completely fill up someone's lap with blessing. When we give generously, we will receive generously.

Being students of the Old Testament, both Jesus and the apostle Paul developed their doctrine of generosity from some of Solomon's wisdom:

> There is one who scatters, yet increases more;
> And there is one who withholds more than is right,
> But it leads to poverty.
> The generous soul will be made rich,
> And he who waters will also be watered himself.
>
> (PROV. 11:24–25)

Paul repeated that idea when he wrote, "He who sows sparingly will also reap sparingly, and he who sows bountifully will also reap bountifully" (2 Cor. 9:6). He concluded,

> Let each one [give] as he has made up his own mind and purposed in his heart, not reluctantly or sorrowfully or under compulsion, for God loves (He takes pleasure in, prizes above other things, and is unwilling to abandon or to do without) a cheerful (joyous, "prompt-to-do-it") giver [whose heart is in his giving]. (2 Cor. 9:7 AMPC)

If we sow sparingly, then we restrict our access to the unlimited wagon of provision and reap at the same level—sparingly. If you don't have a bountiful harvest, consider how much you planted. Sow sparingly, reap sparingly, or sow bountifully, reap bountifully.

Paul also identified that our heart attitudes can hinder our blessings. We shouldn't yield to any kind of compulsion, pressure, or fear. Neither should we give with reluctance or sorrow, but because of the goodness and generosity of God, we should give with generous and purposeful hearts.

Finally, Paul identified God's response to those who give bountifully with the proper heart attitude: God loves a cheerful giver. The Amplified translation in verse 7 above reveals the full meaning of the language Paul used. "God loves (He takes pleasure in, prizes above other things, and is *unwilling to abandon or to do without*) a cheerful (joyous, "prompt-to-do-it") giver [whose heart is in his giving]." I call that a type of spiritual job security. God cannot do without you and will not abandon you when you give in the way Paul described.

In his thank-you letter to the Philippian church, Paul described the significant relationship of giving and receiving he had with their congregation:

And you Philippians know that in the early days of preaching the gospel, after I left Macedonia, no church shared with me in the matter of giving and receiving except you alone; for even in Thessalonica you sent a gift more than once for my needs. Not that I seek the gift itself, but I do seek the profit which increases to your [heavenly] account [the blessing which is accumulating for you]. But I have received everything in full and more; I am amply supplied, having received from Epaphroditus the gifts you sent me. They are the fragrant aroma of an offering, an acceptable sacrifice which God welcomes *and* in which He delights. And my God will liberally supply (fill until full) your every need according to His riches in glory in Christ Jesus. (Phil. 4:15–19 AMP)

Paul described the relationship of giving and receiving that characterized a healthy church relationship. Paul gave to them in the form of spiritual service, and they responded by giving to him in the form of financial aid. Paul was saying, "Since you have given to me, my God will give to you, supplying all your need according to His riches in glory by Christ Jesus."

Knowing that the Lord is generous, merciful, and faithful inspires and encourages us to give freely. Generosity is a primary way to access the blessing of *unlimited provision* contained in the fourth wagon.

Thirteen

THE POWER OF
THE HOLY SPIRIT

A vital connection to the person of the Holy Spirit is essential for the unlimited provision contained in the fourth wagon of my vision to be fully accessed and released in our lives. The apostle Paul wrote, "Now may the God of hope fill you with all joy and peace in believing, that you may abound in hope by the power of the Holy Spirit" (Rom. 15:13).

Our connection to the Holy Spirit must be both powerful and subjective. We fall short of the full empowerment God has provided for us when we settle for a theological knowledge of Him instead of a living relationship, one that energizes, inspires, empowers, and fortifies us. Just before Jesus' ascension He emphasized to His followers the importance of waiting on the Holy Spirit until He came to them in power:

Being assembled together with them, He commanded them not to depart from Jerusalem, but to wait for the Promise of the Father, "which," He said, "you have heard from Me; for John truly baptized with water, but you shall be baptized with the Holy Spirit not many days from now." (Acts 1:4–5)

Our relationship with Him is so vital that Jesus identified the Holy Spirit as "the Promise of the Father." Our relationship with God is based primarily upon His promises. Since God cannot lie, we build our faith by believing those promises. Some have said the Bible contains more than seven thousand promises. But only the Holy Spirit is called "the Promise of the Father"!

The apostles walked, lived, observed, and were instructed by Jesus for more than three years. Yet that experience alone was not enough to prepare them to fulfill their mission. The apostles were afraid of their enemies and locked themselves behind closed doors until after they had a power encounter with the Holy Spirit at Pentecost.

Jesus identified power as the primary characteristic His disciples would experience when the Holy Spirit came to them: "You shall receive power when the Holy Spirit has come upon you" (Acts 1:8). If those who walked with Jesus needed to experience the power of the Holy Spirit the way they did at Pentecost, how much more do you and I, who have not had three-plus years of personal instruction from the Lord Jesus Himself, need this experience!

What did that power look like when the Holy Spirit came? How did it affect Jesus' faithful followers? People who saw what happened described the scene as confusing, amazing, marvelous, and perplexing. Others mocked the proceedings and determined the 120 were drunk on new wine. Peter didn't deny that they were drunk but explained that their behavior was of a different kind of drunkenness.

Friar Raniero Cantalamessa, a leader in the Catholic charismatic renewal, made this remarkable observation:

On the day Pentecost came in fullness the followers of Jesus were filled with the Holy Spirit. We tend to overlook Peter's opening words to the crowd that first Pentecost morning, to our own peril. His denial of drunkenness in the wake of the outpouring of the Holy Spirit should stop us in our tracks. What was going on here? How did the apostles experience the Holy Spirit? What was he teaching them? How was he empowering them? What does this scene in the streets of Jerusalem mean for us today?[1]

Even though the believers' specific behavior is not mentioned, God revealed to Peter that the experience began fulfilling Joel's prophesy from many generations earlier:

> For these are not drunk, as you suppose, since it is only the third hour of the day. But this is what was spoken by the prophet Joel: "And it shall come to pass in the last days, says God, That I will pour out of My Spirit on all flesh; your sons and your daughters shall prophesy, your young men shall see visions, your old men shall dream dreams. And on My menservants and on My maidservants I will pour out My Spirit in those days; and they shall prophesy." (Acts 2:15–18)

That scene was startling, confusing, empowering, and controversial. It still is today. Father Cantalamessa rightfully observed that we deny or denigrate that experience to our own peril. Could it be that such a seemingly foolish experience may actually be the key to living a joyful supernatural life of power? Could it be the missing ingredient in sustaining and empowering a life filled with hope?

How many people have missed the powerful infilling of the Holy Spirit because it seems so foolish? Is there evidence in the Scriptures that God may use seemingly foolish things to accomplish His purpose? Yes, "God has chosen the foolish things of the world to put to shame the wise, and God has chosen the weak things of the world to put to shame the things which are mighty" (1 Cor. 1:27).

God sometimes chooses foolish things to confound natural wisdom and withstand our inclination toward pride and misguided trust in our human understanding. The cross itself, the very basis for our redemption, has been considered by many to be foolish: "The message of the cross is foolishness to those who are perishing, but to us who are being saved it is the power of God. For it is written: 'I will destroy the wisdom of the wise, and bring to nothing the understanding of the prudent'" (1 Cor. 1:18–19).

We can be so dependent upon our human mind-set that when God does something remarkable and different than we expect, we miss it—or even dismiss it. This pattern is evident throughout Scripture.

God appeared to Moses as a fiery-speaking visage from the midst of a burning bush. That startling episode dislodged Moses from his mundane occupation as shepherd into a remarkable role as leader to the Israelite nation, delivering them from four hundred years of Egyptian bondage.

Jesus was born in a stable, not in a palace. His humble birth was not enjoyed or witnessed by significant religious leaders of their time, but the angels announced His coming to a few humble shepherds who were willing to go see the great sight. When Jesus began His miracle ministry, it confused the religious authorities because He came through Judah's family line and not through Levi's priestly lineage. Many Pharisees did not recognize Jesus as the Messiah because He did not act the way they thought a Messiah should. We, too, must be careful not to expect God to do things the way we think He should. We can miss Him too.

The Bible isn't always specifically clear about what happened when the Holy Spirit was poured out. But one thing is clear: there was tangible evidence each time. In many cases the recipients spoke with other tongues, prophesied, appeared to be drunk. Outward manifestations have accompanied outpourings of the Holy Spirit from generation to generation.

INTOXICATING JOY

A predominant characteristic of the Holy Spirit's outpouring is intoxicating joy. Joy is one of three primary components of the kingdom of God: "The kingdom of God is not eating and drinking, but righteousness and peace and joy in the Holy Spirit" (Rom. 14:17). I once read that joy is an infallible sign of the presence of God. Men substitute soberness and intellect for spiritual maturity. Nevertheless, joy is an essential characteristic of a truly spiritual person. Jesus, the most mature of all, "was anointed with the oil of gladness more than his brethren" (Heb. 1:9). *Gladness* means "exceeding joy." Joy is so significant that Jesus died to obtain it: "Looking unto Jesus, the author and finisher of our faith, who *for the joy that was set before Him* endured the cross, despising the shame" (Heb. 12:2).

Down through Christian history, saints expressed the importance of joy. Saint Teresa of Avila specifically warned her sisters against a deadly serious religiosity: "A sad nun is a bad nun. . . . I am more afraid of one unhappy sister than a crowd of evil spirits. . . . What would happen if we hid what little sense of humor we had? Let each of us humbly use this to cheer others."[2] While traveling to one of her convents, she was knocked off her donkey and fell into the mud. She said, "Lord, you couldn't have picked a worse time for this to happen.

Why would you let this happen?" And the response in prayer that she heard was, "That is how I treat my friends." Teresa said, "And that is why you have so few of them!"[3] Her playful way of addressing God assumes God's own playfulness.

James Martin, author and Jesuit priest, wrote:

St. Philip Neri, called The Humorous Saint, hung at his door a little sign: The House of Christian Mirth. Christian joy is a gift from God flowing from a good conscience. A more contemporary example is Pope John XXIII, whose most famous response came when a journalist innocently asked, "Your Holiness, how many people work in the Vatican?" John replied, "About half of them."

Wit is a time-honored way to challenge the pompous, the puffed-up or the powerful. Jesus used humor in this fashion, exposing and defusing the arrogance of religious authorities. Humor can serve as a weapon in the battle against the arrogance and pride that sometimes infect the church. It is also a gentle weapon that can be wielded by the powerless.[4]

THE HOLY SPIRIT'S INTOXICATING INFLUENCE IN THE OLD TESTAMENT

A number of Old Testament scriptures refer to the manifestation of the Spirit and His intoxicating influence. The famous Twenty-Third Psalm identifies what Jesus, our great Shepherd, will do for us today: "You prepare a table before me in the presence of my enemies; You anoint my head with oil; my cup runs over" (v. 5).

However, in the Septuagint (the one the apostles read), "my cup runs over" is translated this way: "Your cup is making me drunk like the finest wine."

The Latin Vulgate translates the phrase "My inebriating chalice, how excellent it is!" or "Your intoxicating cup, how excellent it is!"

"You anoint my head with oil" speaks of the joy of the Holy Spirit affecting our mental disposition. This is an Old Testament expression of what Jesus can do when He gives us the Holy Spirit. Jesus Himself was a recipient and beneficiary of this very same kind of oil. He had an anointing of joy that was first prophesied in Psalm 45:7 and then quoted to describe Him in Hebrews 1:9: "You have loved righteousness and hated lawlessness; therefore God, Your God, has anointed You with the oil of gladness more than Your companions."

Isaiah prophesied a clear picture in the Old Testament of Jesus' New Testament ministry. Jesus preached from those very verses that detail the benefits for those who partake of the gospel, including that oil of joy:

> The Spirit of the Lord God is upon Me,
> Because the Lord has anointed Me
> To preach good tidings to the poor . . .
> To console those who mourn in Zion,
> To give them beauty for ashes,
> The oil of joy for mourning,
> The garment of praise for the spirit of heaviness.
>
> (Isa. 61:1, 3)

The Song of Solomon, also known as the Song of Songs, is often understood as a picture of the love Christ has for His bride. Solomon wrote, "He brought me to the banqueting house, and his banner over me was love" (Song of Solomon 2:4). Some have translated "banqueting house" as "house of wine." The word *banqueting* is a word that literally means "to effervesce as fermented wine, by implication intoxication."[5] The idea is that God's love for us is so strong that when we experience it at a high level, it is intoxicating.

The psalmist David presented a declaration about the Lord's goodness that causes us to trust in Him. It also contains evidence of the intoxicating influence of the Holy Spirit. He wrote,

> How precious is Your lovingkindness, O God!
> Therefore the children of men put their trust under the shadow
> of Your wings.
> They are *abundantly satisfied* with the fullness of Your house,
> And You give them drink from the river of Your pleasures.
> For with You is the fountain of life;
> In Your light we see light.
>
> (Ps. 36:7–9)

"They are abundantly satisfied" is translated "they shall be made drunk" in five ancient translations. The word *and* is not in the original text, thus we see the intoxicating effect of drinking from the river of God's pleasures.

THE HOLY SPIRIT'S INTOXICATING INFLUENCE IN THE NEW TESTAMENT

On the last day of the Feast of Tabernacles, Jesus stood up in the temple and shouted to all who could hear Him,

"If anyone thirsts, let him come to Me and drink. He who believes in Me, as the Scripture has said, out of his heart will flow rivers of living water." But this He spoke concerning the Spirit, whom those believing in Him would receive; for the Holy Spirit was not yet given, because Jesus was not yet glorified. (John 7:37–39)

Jesus clearly promises that He empowers anyone who drinks from Him and that rivers of living water would flow out of them. The author of the gospel of John directly links that experience to being empowered by the Holy Spirit when He would come. One commentary describes what happened on the eighth or last great day of the Feast of Tabernacles as an experience of great joy, a type of what happens when the Holy Spirit is given as we saw in the apostles' experience at Pentecost.

It was a Sabbath, the last feast day of the year, and distinguished by very remarkable ceremonies. "The generally joyous character of this feast," says Olshausen, "broke out on this day into loud jubilation, particularly at the solemn moment when the priest, as was done on every day of this festival, brought forth, in golden vessels, water from the stream of Siloah, which flowed under the temple-mountain, and solemnly poured it upon the altar. Then the words of Isaiah 12:3 were sung, 'With joy shall ye draw water out of the wells of Salvation,' and thus the symbolical reference of this act, intimated in John 7:39, was expressed.'" "So ecstatic," says Lightfoot, "was the joy with which this ceremony was performed— accompanied with sound of trumpets—that it used to be said, 'Whoever had not witnessed it had never seen rejoicing at all.'"[6]

Jesus gave the prerequisite for having this experience: *thirst!* He will meet the deepest cravings in the depths of the hearts of mankind.

The apostle Paul contrasted natural drunkenness with spiritual drunkenness. He very obviously affirmed that natural drunkenness will not satisfy us and is the wrong way to find joy. He wrote, "Do not be drunk with wine, in which is dissipation; but be filled with the Spirit, speaking to one another in psalms and hymns and spiritual songs, singing and making melody in your heart to the Lord, giving thanks always for all things to God the Father in the name of our Lord Jesus Christ" (Eph. 5:18–20).

Thus, being filled with the Spirit may look much like natural drunkenness, with people not only singing but singing *to one another* and exuberantly *giving thanks*. Everyone has needs that cannot be met with the things of this world. Many Christian children have fallen prey to alcoholism and drug addiction because in many churches there has been nothing *spiritual* to drink. The Holy Spirit has become more of an idea or concept than a Person who can satisfy our deepest longings and urges. God has a remedy: *the power of the Holy Spirit.*

I love seeing people touched by the Lord in this empowering and emotional way. Their experiences are precious. Sometimes when the Lord touches people deeply their experience is not one of joy and laughter but manifests instead in weeping and profound healing. That, too, is an aspect of His power being imparted.

One evening I preached on the power of the Holy Spirit using the following two verses from Paul's letter to the Galatians: "This only I want to learn from you: Did you receive the Spirit by the works of the law, or by the hearing of faith?" (3:2); and "Therefore He who supplies the Spirit to you and works miracles among you, does He do it by the works of the law, or by the hearing of faith?" (3:5).

The point of my message was that faith is the only qualifier for encountering the Lord and receiving a miracle from Him. I challenged the congregation to believe God for the specific thing that they needed, and I began to pray for people.

A couple who are dear friends of mine were there that night. They had lost their oldest child in a tragic, fiery car accident. The mother was traumatized by a repetitive oppressive vision of her daughter's charred body and others seeing her daughter in that condition. Her motherly instinct was to protect her daughter from onlookers in that unsightly state. The vision often played over and over in her mind like a broken record, and she was helpless to stop it.

At the end of the meeting that night, several of us prayed for her, and she wept so hard that I was concerned for her. In my mind I heard the enemy say, *See what you've done! You pushed her over the edge and she's losing her mind!* I quietly responded, "She's had forty years to lose her mind, and I've only been praying a few minutes. I'm not quitting!"

My friend stopped sobbing after a while, and I learned that the miracle she sought was to be free of those terrible recurring visions. Since that powerful encounter with the Holy Spirit, she has never been oppressed by that vision again. Jesus healed her that night as we prayed and she wept.

Another mother, whom I will call Jane, experienced healing in a profoundly different way. She and her husband, Matthew, had been in church with me for years when their unmarried teenage daughter got pregnant. When time came for the baby to be born, the couple were in their daughter's hospital room and the baby's father was there. The baby's father and Matthew got into a fight, tussling on the floor, right in the hospital room! Jane struggled to cope with those stressful events and became depressed.

The church I pastored began to experience an outpouring of the Holy Spirit. One of the ways the Spirit touched people manifested as spiritual intoxication, which often resulted as intense laughter. One

Sunday morning at the end of the service I saw Jane sitting on the back row of the sanctuary. I knew she was having a difficult time, and I wanted the Lord to touch her. I asked her if I could pray for her, and as I did she began to laugh and laugh. I mean, she really cackled!

For a long time she laughed hysterically, and her depression instantly left and affected her no longer. She became one of my best intercessors and later began to work for a national Christian ministry, where she thrived for years. That's what the power of the Spirit can do. It may look foolish, but the fruit is indisputable. God will do foolish things to confound the wise and bless His children in the process.

Some have criticized these outpourings of joy, prominent during the 1990s, that sometimes inundated entire congregations. They believe those experiences are not scriptural. But consider these verses from the Psalms:

> When the LORD brought back the captivity of Zion,
> We were like those who dream.
> Then our mouth was filled with laughter,
> And our tongue with singing.
> Then they said among the nations,
> "The LORD has done great things for them."
> The LORD has done great things for us,
> And we are glad.
>
> (126:1–3)

Everyone agrees that corporate singing is proper, but consider that corporate laughter may be as well. In the phrase "our mouth was filled with laughter," *our* is plural and *mouth* is singular. That means that the corporate mouth of the congregation was as filled with laughter as was their corporate tongue filled with singing. That Old Testament image clearly portrays this New Testament experience.

Zechariah prophesied something very similar when he said, "Those of Ephraim shall be like a mighty man, and their heart shall rejoice as if with wine. Yes, their children shall see it and be glad; their heart shall rejoice in the LORD" (Zech. 10:7).

These verses speak of a corporate rejoicing for the great things the Lord has done. The experience shall encourage the next generation to rejoice in the Lord also.

GOD'S PRESENCE

The presence of the Lord has a particular influence on people. David said, "You will show me the path of life; in Your presence is fullness of joy" (Ps. 16:11). The path of life leads us into the presence of the Lord. God's presence can be so intense that you may experience joy so powerfully it can render you speechless, as the apostle Peter wrote, "Though now you do not see Him, yet believing, you rejoice with joy inexpressible and full of glory" (1 Peter 1:8). The book of Job affirms the same truth: "He will yet fill your mouth with laughing, and your lips with rejoicing" (Job 8:21).

Joy and gladness are indispensable fruits of the Spirit and aspects of His empowerment. We can sustain lives of joy as we are continually filled with the Holy Spirit. We have a part to play. What He does for us will not always happen automatically. The psalm declares, "Oh, taste and see that the LORD is good; blessed is the man who trusts in Him!" (Ps. 34:8). Later in the Gospels Jesus explained that living water will flow not just into us but out of us if we would but come to Him thirsty and drink from Him by faith (John 7:37–38). The Holy Spirit is not just a force or thing but a Person who wants to empower us to live lives of power. He is the One who sustains our hope!

Part Six

Wagon Five: A New Vision for the United States

Fourteen

DRAW NEAR TO GOD

The fifth and final wagon in my encounter was filled with *a new vision for our nation*. God has a new vision for the United States much different from its current condition. The first four wagons contained divine substance that, on the surface, seemed to be only for individuals. But collectively those provisions, appropriated and lived out in individual believers, have the capacity to awaken our nation to a new era of spiritual and societal greatness.

In the Bible text, Jacob was in a state of despair before Joseph sent the wagons to get him. He believed his favorite son Joseph was dead and his entire family was in danger of destruction. But suddenly everything changed. When he discovered that Joseph was alive and saw the wagons provided for his family's escape to abundance in Egypt, Jacob revived.

Jacob is a picture of many believers in our nation who need a renewed sense of purpose and destiny. Joseph is a type of the Lord Jesus, the One who was dead but is not only alive but Lord of all. The analogy speaks of God's heart to restore the church and our nation through a transformational awakening. Because of the relationship

Joseph had with Pharaoh, Jacob's family was given Goshen as their new home, the best place to live in all Egypt. One missing key to this restoration is found in the meaning of the word *Goshen*.

Pharaoh instructed Joseph, "The land of Egypt is before you. Have your father and brothers dwell in the best of the land; let them dwell in the land of Goshen" (Gen. 47:6). *Goshen* means "to draw near." Jewish Old Testament scholars conclude it came from a root word meaning "relationship," or "bridge between two parties." *Goshen* speaks of a relational bridge enabling two parties to draw near to each other.

A new vision for our nation depends on our heart response in drawing near to God. Scripture says, "Draw near to God and He will draw near to you. Cleanse your hands, you sinners; and purify your hearts, you double-minded" (James 4:8).

This verse connects the idea of drawing near with repentance from sin and changing our minds. Repentance is not just turning from sin, but it completes itself in turning toward God. Too often we focus on turning from the sin and neglect the part that completes the transaction, turning to the Father Himself.

Jesus came to restore our relationship with our heavenly Father. He proclaimed, "Repent, for the kingdom of heaven is at hand" (Matt. 4:17). He preached repentance as the way to experience the kingdom. He offered a positive reason to turn from sin by providing an alternative lifestyle much more wonderful than one of negativity and self-centeredness. Being self-focused is the landing pad for demonic oppression. True repentance becomes a reorientation of our mind and life, from one dominated by self-centeredness to a life of God-centeredness. Through Him we may participate in a kingdom that changes lives and expands exponentially our capacity to change the world. We must turn our focus away from ourselves and toward God and His kingdom.

What's Your Focus?

Jacob's life story is a peculiar one that illustrates the importance of focus. Jacob worked for his uncle, who continually cheated him out of his just wages. Jacob offered to continue tending Laban's herds as long as he retained ownership of all brown, streaked, speckled, and spotted sheep and goats. Laban agreed to his offer, so Jacob took those animals and tended them, but he did an unusual thing:

> Now Jacob took for himself rods of green poplar and of the almond and chestnut trees, peeled white strips in them, and exposed the white which was in the rods. And the rods which he had peeled, he set before the flocks in the gutters, in the watering troughs where the flocks came to drink, so that they should conceive when they came to drink. So the flocks conceived before the rods, and the flocks brought forth streaked, speckled, and spotted. (Gen. 30:37–39)

In the watering trough, which was also the place of reproduction, Jacob set before the flocks peeled almond and chestnut rods with white strips in them. As a result, the sheep and goats gave birth to animals exclusively spotted and streaked. Those sheep and goats became Jacob's property and made him a wealthy man. How that happened in the natural is quite mysterious. There is a spiritual message in it though: we will reproduce whatever captures our imagination, whatever our minds focus on. The writer of the book of Hebrews encouraged us to be "looking unto Jesus, the author and finisher of our faith" (Heb. 12:2). If we focus on our sinfulness instead of gazing upon the One to whom we turned, our old nature will try to hold us in bondage.

Jesus promised to those who "seek first the kingdom of God

and His righteousness" that all other things would be added to them (Matt. 6:33). As Jesus focused first on the kingdom and pleasing His Father, He transformed the immediate society around Him through wisdom, insight, and demonstrations of supernatural power, unusual signs, wonders, and miracles. Those who followed His example to seek first the kingdom experienced the same transformation.

As believers in our nation draw near to God in an unprecedented magnitude, He will draw near to us in a reciprocal way. There will be such a visible drawing near of our God that we will see whole cities in the United States radiating with the glory, presence, and power of God in ways we cannot yet imagine. Lord, show us Your glory!

Our Time to Shine!

In the darkest of times God commands us to arise and shine:

> Arise, shine;
> For your light has come!
> And the glory of the LORD is risen upon you.
> For behold, the darkness shall cover the earth,
> And deep darkness the people;
> But the LORD will arise over you,
> And His glory will be seen upon you.
> The Gentiles shall come to your light,
> And kings to the brightness of your rising.
>
> (ISA. 60:1–3)

He knows better than we do what He has already deposited within us. And as we arise and shine He will arise over us, and His glory will be seen upon us, even when darkness covers the earth and deep darkness many people. Those days are upon us now.

THE ULTIMATE PURPOSE OF THE ANOINTING

The ultimate purpose of the Holy Spirit's anointing is the restoration of cities and family legacies. Jesus' first recorded sermon originated from Isaiah 61 and accurately described the main characteristics of His ministry and should describe ours too.

> "The Spirit of the Lord GOD is upon Me,
> Because the LORD has anointed Me
> To preach good tidings to the poor;
> He has sent Me to heal the brokenhearted,
> To proclaim liberty to the captives,
> And the opening of the prison to those who are bound;
> To proclaim the acceptable year of the LORD,
> And the day of vengeance of our God;
> To comfort all who mourn,
> To console those who mourn in Zion,
> To give them beauty for ashes,
> The oil of joy for mourning,
> The garment of praise for the spirit of heaviness;
> That they may be called trees of righteousness,
> The planting of the LORD, that He may be glorified."

> And they shall rebuild the old ruins,
> They shall raise up the former desolations,
> And they shall repair the ruined cities,
> The desolations of many generations.
> Strangers shall stand and feed your flocks,

And the sons of the foreigner
Shall be your plowmen and your vinedressers.
But you shall be named the priests of the LORD,
They shall call you the servants of our God.
You shall eat the riches of the Gentiles,
And in their glory you shall boast.

(ISA. 61:1–6)

Jesus carried the manifest presence of God. He was anointed to preach good news with such power that lives were changed dramatically. The recipients would become oaks of righteousness as God's special planting that the great God might receive glory. But that was not all. Those fully restored by the anointing would "rebuild the old ruins," "raise up the former desolations," and "repair the ruined cities"—the "desolations of many generations." All these wonderful benefits and promises were contained in a special period of time: the acceptable year of the Lord.

JUBILEE

In its early history, Israel was authorized by the Lord to observe a special celebration every fifty years called the year of Jubilee. Jesus called it "the acceptable year of the Lord." *Jubilee* literally means "a clamorous acclamation of joy," typified by the victorious joyful blowing of the shofar. The Bible describes the original intent of that year of Jubilee:

You shall consecrate the fiftieth year, and proclaim liberty throughout all the land to all its inhabitants. It shall be a Jubilee for you;

and each of you shall return to his possession, and each of you shall return to his family. That fiftieth year shall be a Jubilee to you; in it you shall neither sow nor reap what grows of its own accord, nor gather the grapes of your untended vine. . . .

And if one of your brethren who dwells by you becomes poor, and sells himself to you, you shall not compel him to serve as a slave. As a hired servant and a sojourner he shall be with you, and shall serve you until the Year of Jubilee. And then he shall depart from you—he and his children with him —and shall return to his own family. He shall return to the possession of his fathers. (Lev. 25:10–11, 39–41)

How could the year of Jubilee not be joyous? That year all property was returned to the original owner. Any slave or indentured servant was set free along with his entire family. All debts were forgiven to assure that no family would abide in perpetual poverty.

When Jesus declared the "acceptable year of the Lord," He enforced the reality of the original Jubilee year by the power of the anointing and the Holy Spirit's work: "good news for the poor" as well as "freedom for the captives." History does not record that Israel ever celebrated a year of Jubilee. Jesus came to enact that Jubilee, not one that occurs every fifty years, but a permanent one that continues to this day.

The Priesthood and Spiritual Fathers

Prior to and during Isaiah's prophetic tenure, only those born in the tribe of Levi were eligible to be priests, yet he declared, "You shall be named the priests of the LORD" (Isa. 61:6). I am sure Isaiah disturbed the established priesthood with that radical proclamation. The word *named* means "to call out," "to call by name," or "to appoint." When we were born again we were born into a new family, the Father's family, and He has *named* us as both kings and priests. Our Father has created a new family lineage, wherein all his sons and daughters are priests. The anointing of the Holy Spirit is the effective enabling agent whereby we exercise the very priesthood that Isaiah prophesied.

Yes, Scripture assures us we are all priests by virtue of our new birth as children of God: "As many as received Him, to them He gave the right to become children of God, to those who believe in His name: who were born, not of blood, nor of the will of the flesh, nor of the will of man, but of God" (John 1:12–13); and "You are a chosen generation, a royal priesthood, a holy nation, His own special people, that you may proclaim the praises of Him who called you out of darkness into His marvelous light; who once were not a people but are now the people of God, who had not obtained mercy but now have obtained mercy" (1 Peter 2:9–10).

These priests embody a lifestyle permeated with the manifest presence of God. They will walk in aspects of the Isaiah 61 anointing, just as our forerunner Jesus. This priesthood will continually release the reality, deliverance, hope, and restoration that the original year of Jubilee promised.

PRESENCE-BASED COMMUNITIES

Jesus inaugurated a *presence*-based community of people equipped to rebuild the old ruins, raise up the former desolations, and repair the ruined cities, the desolations of many generations described in Isaiah 61:4. Not only will this anointing restore deteriorated cities, but it will also restore the spiritual legacies of families disenfranchised, perhaps even for generations. Is it possible that the anointing of the Holy Spirit is sufficient to restore to our generation what has been lost over the years? Yes! We have believed for much too little. We must set our sights much higher than ever before.

When Joseph sent the wagons from Egypt to Jacob, Jacob's heart revived. The once-despondent patriarch was so shocked and blessed that upon embracing the full impact of his deliverance he said, "It is enough. Joseph my son is still alive. I will go and see him before I die" (Gen. 45:28).

The phrase "It is enough" is not translated very well in the New King James version. It originates from a word that signifies "multitude or abundance." Jacob most likely exclaimed, "This is more than I could have ever imagined!" Jacob responded much as Paul the apostle did centuries later when he saw the fullness of the gospel of Christ and said, "Now to Him who is able to do exceedingly abundantly above all that we ask or think, according to the power that works in us" (Eph. 3:20).

That is exactly what we exclaim, too, when our eyes are opened and our imaginations are energized by the goodness of God.

THE ANOINTING

The purpose of the anointing is not simply to have great meetings or only see people healed and delivered. We are called to establish Holy Spirit presence-based communities of people with the potential to restore whole cities. The ultimate goal of the anointing in the lives of believers is to transform society. We may be satisfied in making a few disciples, but Jesus has called us to disciple whole nations (Matt. 28:19).

We have the potential for an ongoing experience of outpoured glory and an encounter with God that has a greater purpose than we have ever imagined. The purpose is to fuel a national awakening to transform the United States. To see ourselves as a post-Christian nation is a defeatist mentality. Having had Christian roots in the founding of our nation is not the same thing as being a Christian nation. We may in fact be a pre-Christian nation. Don't settle for less than believing for the Lord to do His greatest work on our behalf in this generation.

Our best days lie ahead!

— *Fifteen* —

THE POWER OF FORGIVENESS

Forgiveness is key to unlocking the floodgates of the abundance contained in the five wagons of my vision. Receiving forgiveness is but one part of the equation. We must extend forgiveness to everyone who has offended or wounded us. This, too, is an important part of drawing near to God. John the apostle wrote, "If someone says, 'I love God,' and hates his brother, he is a liar; for he who does not love his brother whom he has seen, how can he love God whom he has not seen? And this commandment we have from Him: that he who loves God must love his brother also" (1 John 4:20–21).

A pivotal passage in the Lord's Prayer is the hinge upon which heaven's doors swing wide open:

Forgive us our debts, as we forgive our debtors. And do not lead us into temptation, but deliver us from the evil one. For Yours is the kingdom and the power and the glory forever. Amen. For if you forgive men their trespasses, your heavenly Father will also forgive you. But if you do not forgive men their trespasses, neither will your heavenly Father forgive your trespasses.

(MATT. 6:12–15)

A little boy whose Sunday school teacher asked him to recite the Lord's Prayer said it best: "And forgive us our trash passes as we forgive those who pass trash against us." His recitation wasn't exactly on point, but the spirit of his words was spot-on. He understood that to forgive people he must stop passing on their trash to others. We know we truly forgive someone when we stop talking about what they did to us. Forgiveness at its simplest means no trash passing allowed!

FORGIVENESS IS CRUCIAL FOR A NEW VISION

Forgiveness is also crucial to the fulfillment of a new vision for our nation. Our bitterness and sinful behavior affect even the land, the environment, and the weather patterns. Paul made this profound observation:

> The earnest expectation of the creation eagerly waits for the revealing of the sons of God. For the creation was subjected to futility, not willingly, but because of Him who subjected it in hope; because the creation itself also will be delivered from the bondage of corruption into the glorious liberty of the children of God. (Rom. 8:19–21)

Nature itself was made subject to futility because of the fall of Adam, meaning that the earth has been hindered from living up to its full potential and original purpose. Nevertheless, God preserved creation's future by also imprisoning it in hope, as the text states: "Because of Him who subjected it in hope." Creation itself responds to hope-filled people. The curse affecting the planet will reverse in response to people who live in true harmony with God. The quality of the seasons, the soil, the growth cycles, the size and quality of fruit, the atmosphere, and the seas will all improve. Hope is a primary key that opens the door to life on our planet as God intended it.

BREAKING THE CURSE OF RACIAL HATRED

Jim Hill, an American missionary to Argentina and longtime trusted friend, experienced this truth firsthand. He witnessed an episode of reconciliation between Argentine Christians and Native Americans that literally changed the climate of a region called the Impenetrable, an area of the Grand Chaco plain. He gives the following account abbreviated from his book, *Impenetrable: Breaking the Curse of Racial Hatred*. It is a message we should all heed for the welfare of our nation:

> By the 1800s the Native American tribes and descendants of European colonists in South America had been in conflict for centuries. Both sides committed atrocities, but the Native Americans suffered the most fatalities. As Europeans continued to immigrate and new generations of their descendants were born, these white men had an insatiable appetite for more and more land.
>
> Right in the center of the continent lies a large geographical region known as the Gran Chaco. For generations the Wichi, Toba, Mocoví, Mataco, Abipone, and Pilagá tribes made this area their homeland, but the encroachment of settlers and farmers became inevitable.
>
> Tribal tradition reveals that many of their leaders and shamans realized the whites would soon possess all the good land. They decided to curse their own territory to make it unfruitful. They hoped the white man would not want a land so barren and uninhabitable. The tribal leaders concluded that even a cursed land would be better than having no land of their own.

As the settlers advanced toward the center of the Gran Chaco, they encountered an area where everything had a thorn, or a stinger, and so little rain fell that they could not grow crops. Trees with six-inch thorns grew in the middle of dried up riverbeds where fish once swam. Even the few remaining Wichí and Toba could not hunt and fish as successfully as they once had, but at least they had a place to call home.

Then on September 13, 1884, the Argentine government passed a decree openly stating their intent to kill, drive out, or subjugate as forced laborers all Indians in the Chaco. The government appointed Benjamín Victorica as commandant of the army's expeditionary force authorizing him to eliminate the Indian problem by any means necessary. Authorities charged him with opening up the territory for civilization.

With stubborn tenacity the few remaining tribes resisted. The land itself seemed to resist the army's advances. The soldiers began to call the region "El Impenetrable" because they could neither penetrate nor subjugate it. All attempts for total elimination of the Indians failed. Both sides in the conflict lost many lives.

These misguided policies bore the fruit of distrust, bitterness, and racial hatred. Armed conflicts, even massacres continued in the Chaco as late as the 1920s and 1930s with each group blaming the other. The pools of bitterness deepened as the waters of the rivers continued to dry up.

God had a plan to bring health and healing to this place known as the Impenetrable. The Lord revealed to me and several other Argentine pastors that He wanted to reconcile the long and painful divide between the Argentine Christians and Native Americans. Local leaders developed a plan and chose a place to initiate a time of reconciliation. I lived in the United States at the time and traveled to Argentina for the express purpose of participating in this event.

When I arrived at the airport in Resistencia, my friend Alberto was waiting for me. He took me to his home, where I would be staying. Over the supper table we began to talk about our trip out to the Impenetrable. He filled me in on some of the behind the scenes details I hadn't heard before.

The idea for the reconciliation meeting between tribal leaders and European descent church leaders was birthed at a Bible Training School located in the village of Nueva Pompeya.

One morning the pastor taught on the Bible passage about the time Jesus washed His disciples' feet. In the middle of his teaching he felt a strong conviction that he should also wash his students' feet. The students were all Wichí and Toba tribal leaders.

As the pastor knelt before them he began to weep and ask forgiveness for all of the sins Argentine Christians committed against the Native Americans.

The pastor's act of humility and request for forgiveness so touched the tribal leaders that they also repented for the actions of their ancestors. In that moment they experienced a remarkable sense of God's love, and an outpouring of the power of the Holy Spirit.

A flood of liberating forgiveness and healing for the wounds of bitterness, suspicion, and resentment filled their hearts. They decided that they should call a solemn public assembly so that the whole community could experience this newfound freedom. They also wanted to reject the ancient curses that their ancestors had spoken over the land, and ask God to pour out His blessings from heaven.

They set a significant date for the reconciliation assembly.

They would gather on the eve of the anniversary of the historic 1884 decree authorizing the extermination of all Native Americans in the Chaco. Word spread quickly. People from thousands of miles away heard of the assembly and decided to participate. Teams organized to converge on Nueva Pompeya from the north, south, east, and west.

Each team had representatives from the Argentine Churches and tribal leaders from as far away as the USA. The leading pastors decided to stop at all the remote villages along the way to repent to any Native Americans they could find, asking for their forgiveness. The event took on a life of its own, growing far beyond the expectations the little group at the Bible School had envisioned.

At the assembly a pastor spoke on the power of forgiveness, and the moderator came to the microphone again. He invited the leaders from six tribal nations, along with the pastors who had been chosen to represent the European descent churches, to come up onto the platform. The tribal leaders then did something totally unexpected.

The Wichí leader took the microphone and said to the Toba leader, "Long before the white men came our peoples were at war. We hated, killed, and raided each other for many generations, but now we are all of the same blood. We believe in the blood of Jesus. We are all a part of His tribe, and we follow Him. We are now blood brothers. I ask you to forgive my people for what we did to your people."

Each of the six tribal leaders in turn, asked and received forgiveness from the other five. They did not hurry as the leaders sought forgiveness and reconciliation. It took quite some time.

When the time came for the white churches to ask forgiveness of the Native Americans a remarkable silence settled on the crowd.

The sense of God's presence must have been intense on the platform, because not one of the pastors thought to use a microphone. No one did anything for show. We saw the tribal leaders gather around the pastors in a circle, lay their hands on them, and bow their heads in prayer.

After several minutes they began to embrace each other and the moderator reappeared on the platform. He invited one of the musical groups to come back to lead the assembly in some songs of praise.

Before the group could plug in their instruments and begin, the wind began to blow. Up until that moment not even a breeze stirred the whole day long. One of those little mini twisters we called dust devils began to form at the back of the plaza. It started just a couple of feet high, but steadily grew larger as it danced down the aisle toward the stage. By the time it reached and engulfed the platform it must have been over twenty feet tall and whirled full tilt. The dust became so thick you could barely keep your eyes open. The band made a brief attempt to play some music, but when the Argentine flag, the Christian flag, and the large banner with the fish symbol on it went flying off into the trees everyone scurried for cover.

In the midst of all the confusion everyone looked for a place to escape what became a gale force wind. My team jumped into our truck to leave. By the time we reached the paved road in Castelli flashes of lightning filled the dark sky back toward Nueva Pompeya. We arrived at a Baptist church where we were scheduled to spend the night. The pastor and his family prepared a light supper for us of locally baked bread, mortadella, and cheese. As we sat down to eat, it began to rain, not just a gentle rain but a deluge. The sound of the rain on the metal roof was so loud we had to shout so we could hear each other.

The torrential rain continued to pound the metal roof throughout the night. Lightning strikes and crashes of thunder rumbled on for much longer than normal. It was as if the heavens themselves were being shaken and rearranged. The fierce storm that brought the meeting to an abrupt conclusion drenched everything.

There had been no rain during the fifty weeks leading up to the reconciliation meeting. It rained almost every week for the next year. Some may say that was just coincidental. Others may insist it was an unusual natural phenomenon. I believe it was a miracle. Before I left the U.S. for Argentina, back in my home church, I asked for prayer for the journey. During our prayer time a friend of mine gave me a prophetic word. He said to me, "When the curse is broken, run, for the rains are coming." That's why we jumped in our truck and left when the winds began blowing so violently. I know God answered our cries and sent the rain in response to the special reconciliation we all experienced.

Alejandro, one of the pastors who had been part of the reconciliation meeting, returned to Nueva Pompeya a few months later. While he was there he bought a watermelon that was so big he couldn't put it into the trunk of his car by himself. It took two grown men to lift and load it.

What makes this remarkable is that for many years the harvests had been so poor there was never anything to sell.

Since the reconciliation took place, truckloads of farm produce are regularly shipped from the Impenetrable to Resistencia, Castelli, Formosa, and other major cities. Wholesale vegetable companies now send their trucks on established routes throughout the region to buy directly from the farmers.

When we align ourselves with God's heart, walking in forgiveness and mercy, we can expect the favor of God to manifest itself openly in our lives. Something cosmically powerful is released through the transaction of giving and receiving forgiveness for the deepest wounds we have suffered. It changes everything. This principle is not only true and applicable in our personal lives, but is equally true in a much broader sense for people groups, communities, and nations.

In the Impenetrable I saw the effect of this spiritual principle clearly demonstrated over a specific geographical region. Within a few short months after this level of reconciliation occurred, the government announced plans to build a hospital, a high school, and public housing. These projects weren't upgrades or additions to what had previously existed. Prior to the event the nearest high school or hospital was two or three hours away, and most people didn't have personal transportation to get there.[1]

Jim told me concerning this remarkable experience: "I have seen the changes with my own eyes. Before the reconciliation I stood in a dry riverbed with banks at least eight feet high and forty feet across with seventy-five-year-old trees standing in the middle of it. After the reconciliation that same river flowed with water from frequent rains, and many of the trees are waterlogged and dying."

Our land is also in need of a transforming experience of forgiveness and reconciliation between many factions of people. In recent years the polarization of our culture has increased to an alarming degree. Racial, political, and ethnic strife has ripped and torn the very fabric of our society. We must realize that hating haters is still hatred. We cannot conquer works of the flesh with other fleshly means. The deception of self-righteousness that often exists on both sides of the arguments is a grave concern. Such constant negativity, criticism, and hostility opens wide the door to demonic oppression and jeopardizes the futures of those who participate in such unredemptive ways. Forgiveness must prevail if we are to experience the great awakening our nation so desperately needs. Christians must lead the way. It is high time for us to arise and shine!

THE NEXT
GREAT AWAKENING

Sixteen

THE COMING HARVEST

God's intervention in the lives of nations is not relegated to Bible history alone. Our own nation, the United States, has been dramatically impacted by His influence. The Second Great Awakening that began in 1797 at the Red River Meeting House in Logan County, Kentucky, is one such example. After months of spending whole nights of prayer in the woods for a spiritual revival, an outpouring of the Holy Spirit began at Pastor James McGready's small church. McGready described their initial encounter this way: "A mighty effusion of God's Spirit came upon the people and the floor was soon covered with the slain; their screams for mercy pierced the heavens."[1] Thus God initiated a new era of spiritual outpouring that ultimately reshaped the history of the young nation.

After the initial experience, McGready and other leaders planned a camp meeting at the Gasper River Church. A crowd numbering more than eight thousand attended, and many lives were changed forever by the overwhelming power of God. As the activity of God increased, so did the crowds. The largest camp meeting, held at Cane Ridge, drew crowds estimated at between fifteen and twenty thousand. To put this in perspective, Lexington, the largest city in the state, had a population of only eighteen hundred people. Within months the revival spread through Tennessee, North and South Carolina, Virginia, and Pennsylvania. Its lasting impact inspired societal change, increased people's awareness of the needs of the poor, began movements that eventually resulted in the end of slavery, initiated women's right to vote, and dramatically increased the size and influence of the church. God can do it again.

Prophetic encounters over several years have convinced me that our nation will experience yet another great spiritual awakening. The first encounter involved the promises Amos described in the ninth chapter of his prophecy. Verses 11 through 15 describe a time of harvest of unparalleled proportions that will occur in the historic era when God restores the ancient homeland to the Jewish people:

> "On that day I will raise up
> The tabernacle of David, which has fallen down,
> And repair its damages;
> I will raise up its ruins,
> And rebuild it as in the days of old;
> That they may possess the remnant of Edom,
> And all the Gentiles who are called by My name,"
> Says the LORD who does this thing.

> "Behold, the days are coming," says the LORD,
> "When the plowman shall overtake the reaper,
> And the treader of grapes him who sows seed;
> The mountains shall drip with sweet wine,
> And all the hills shall flow with it.
> I will bring back the captives of My people Israel;
> They shall build the waste cities and inhabit them;

They shall plant vineyards and drink wine from them;

They shall also make gardens and eat fruit from them.

I will plant them in their land,

And no longer shall they be pulled up

From the land I have given them,"

Says the LORD your God.

(AMOS 9:11–15)

This short passage describes many aspects of this supernatural harvest. The seedbed for harvest is David's restored tabernacle, groups of people devoted to twenty-four-hour worship with the manifest presence of God in their midst. All over our nation and other parts of the world, this idea has taken root.

The focus of this impending harvest is the Gentile world, which speaks of the nations. This ingathering is so great that it will impact nations.

This awakening shall be an outpouring of intoxicating joy. The mountains, a type of the nations, shall drip with new wine. Like the early disciples at Pentecost who were accused of being drunk when filled with the Holy Spirit, so shall many drink the new wine that flows down upon the hills of humanity.

Amos prophesied, "I will bring back the captives of My people Israel." The restoration of the Jewish people to their historic homeland is a prophetic clock that identifies the timing and generation for this harvest. In 1948 Israel became a nation again after almost two thousand years. That was both unexpected and all but impossible. Never before had a people group lost their geographical home only to regain it many generations later. The prophetic clock for the end-time outpouring began ticking then!

BLANK CHECK FOR REVIVAL

I grew up in an era and in a denomination that never mentioned revival and very few people believed the miraculous power of God was still available. I had no foundation for believing in an end-time revival. As a pastor in that state of doubt back in 1994, the Lord opened my eyes to these prophetic insights and encouraged me to preach them, particularly from Amos 9:13. But I had a problem. I was not yet convinced.

I remember walking the block early one Sunday morning and speaking to the Lord about my reluctance to proclaim the outpouring He urged me to declare from Amos 9:13. As I rounded the corner and headed down the home stretch I noticed a scrap of paper on the side of the road. Immediately I had this clear impression from the Lord: *Pick up that piece of paper.* I stooped to pick it up and discovered it was a partially torn check, number 913, written to a church! It suddenly dawned on me that the very verse I was wrestling with was Amos 9:13. It read: "Behold, the days are coming," says the LORD, "when the plowman shall overtake the reaper, and the treader of grapes him who sows seed; the mountains shall drip with sweet wine, and all the hills shall flow with it."

Check number 913!

The check was a prophetic sign to the church. The Lord had written a blank check for revival, secured in a spiritual safe deposit box—His Word, Amos 9:13! A check is a promissory note. It isn't money but represents the existence and promise of money. I understood that the devil had attempted to tear it up, but the money was still in the bank. God's promise is still good even though it has been torn, tattered, assailed by the enemy, and ignored by the unbelief of mankind.

A great harvest lies before us. God has given us a "blank check" that has been maligned and largely ignored, yet the proverbial *money*, representing the power and intent of God, has been safely guarded by the Lord Himself. Yes, those days are coming!

BACK TO THE FUTURE: THE CHANGE AT HAND

On November 22, 2005, I turned on my new Treo smartphone to check my daily schedule and discovered that the calendar had reverted to 1904. I manually reset the PDA, hoping the calendar would remain at 2005, but once again the 1904 calendar returned. At first I thought my phone was broken, but then I realized the Lord was drawing my attention to the year 1904. I reset the PDA once more. The correct calendar year returned to the screen and never again returned to 1904 or any other incorrect year. I believe the Lord revealed to me that in some way He was going to turn back our calendars to 1904.

The next day after paying for my meal at a local restaurant, I discovered two wheat pennies in my change, one dated 1947 and the other 1951. Wheat pennies were made from 1909 to 1958 and displayed two ears of wheat on the back with "one cent" stamped between them. Above the wheat and across the top is written *E Pluribus Unum*, Latin for "Out of Many, One," a phrase referring to the United States being one nation comprised of many states, or one people comprised of many ethnic groups. The profile of Abraham Lincoln dominates the front side of the coin. Finding one of these pennies in my change is unusual, but finding two at the same time is highly unlikely. For the second time the Lord highlighted years to me, 1947 and 1951. I concluded there must be a message in the three years 1904, 1947, and 1951.

The Lord first got my attention through my phone because He wanted to *communicate* with me. He had my number! The name Treo is a play on the word *trio* meaning "three." This speaks of the Godhead—Father, Son, and Holy Spirit—and coincides with His drawing my attention to the *three* specific years: 1904, 1947, and 1951. The initials PDA can also stand for "public display of affection." A spiritual outpouring is His own unique public display of affection for a lost world in a seemingly hopeless situation.

In each of these years there were major revivals in parts of the world—Wales in 1904, the United States and Canada in 1947, and Argentina in 1951. Why would the Lord speak to me through a computerized calendar that reverted to 1904? Because we are going back to the future! *Our* future holds outpourings like those of 1904, 1947, and 1951. Why did the Lord use the change in my hand to speak to me about those years? Because *a major spiritual change is at hand.* This imminent spiritual season will contain characteristics and power like God poured out in all three of those revivals.

The details on the Lincoln wheat pennies offer a prophetic picture of the characteristics of this revival. The gospel will be proclaimed with authority and with society-changing power. Abraham Lincoln's Emancipation Proclamation in part stated: "All persons held as slaves within any State . . . shall be . . . thenceforward, and forever free; and the Executive Government of the United States, including the military and naval authority thereof, will recognize and maintain the freedom of such persons."[2]

Lincoln's proclamation did not so much free the slaves as proclaim the fact that they were free. Our nation's Declaration of Independence already affirmed that all people are created equal, an inalienable right given by God Himself. The gospel, too, proclaims freedom, but of a different sort. It maintains that the death, burial, and resurrection of the Lord Jesus *have already* set all men free. But many don't know it.

During the American Civil War there were more than four million enslaved African Americans. After Lincoln's proclamation, more than two hundred thousand former slaves joined the Union Armed Forces. The emancipated became emancipators. This is a picture of the coming harvest of souls, where the evangelized become those who evangelize many others. Some have said that when the next outpouring begins, many will believe it is the last one because of the numbers of people being saved. However, it is but the first phase, a *harvesting of the harvesters* for the final, much greater ingathering to follow, much like the *emancipating of the emancipators* in the American Civil War.

My attention was drawn to the wheat on the pennies. Wheat speaks of harvest. When Jesus spoke to the Samaritan woman at Jacob's well, He equated wheat with a harvest of people:

Do you not say, "There are still four months and then comes the harvest"? Behold, I say to you, lift up your eyes and look at the fields, for they are already white for harvest! And he who reaps receives wages, and gathers fruit for eternal life, that both he who sows and he who reaps may rejoice together. For in this the saying is true: "One sows and another reaps." I sent you to reap that for which you have not labored; others have labored, and you have entered into their labors.

And many of the Samaritans of that city believed in Him because of the word of the woman who testified, "He told me all that I ever did." (John 4:35–39)

Many Samaritans were *harvested* as a result of the testimony of the woman Jesus helped. Just as the wheat pennies have "one cent" set between them, many like the woman at the well will be *ones sent* into the harvest in the coming days. This kind of evangelism was common in the 1904 Welsh Revival, when more than one hundred thousand souls were saved in nine months. By 1954, in the Argentine Revival, one single meeting filled a soccer stadium in Buenos Aires with more than 180,000 people who came to hear the gospel. In like manner, during the revivals of the late 1940s and early 1950s, Oral Roberts, Jack Coe, and others traveled the nation attracting many thousands to their healing tent meetings.

The inscription on the back of the coin, *E Pluribus Unum*, meaning "Out of Many, One," is also on the Great Seal of the United States. It is a description of our great country, being many states, united as one. I believe this detail on the penny also represents a picture of a characteristic of the coming harvest. I believe that segments of the body of Christ will enter a new level of unity in the midst of this ingathering of souls. New alliances and allegiances will be formed to harvest the great numbers the Lord is calling in.

The potential of this coming harvest is of a magnitude that will be too broad for any single person or institution to control. Only the Lord Jesus, the true Head of the church, will be able to lead it. This outpouring will be like a mighty moving river that we will need to adapt to. It will take many people working together to fulfill the commission of that day.

WELSH REVIVAL OF 1904

My PDA twice returned my calendar to 1904, the date of one of the most amazing outpourings in recorded history. The Welsh Revival of 1904 is tied to Evan Roberts, a young zealous believer. He grew up in a Christian home and felt the call to preach from a young age. Simultaneously, Seth Joshua, a pastor with the Forward Movement, asked God for many years to raise up a young man from the mines or fields who could lead a revival in Wales. God found that man in young Evan Roberts.

In the days preceding the Welsh Revival, the Lord repeatedly awakened Roberts at 1:00 a.m. to pray for revival. On September 29, Roberts attended a meeting where he heard Pastor Joshua pray that God would bend those in attendance, meaning He would touch them in such a way that they would yield to His power and purpose. Young Evan prayed fervently that God would bend him. God truly answered his prayer.

By the end of October God began to move in many lives as Roberts stood in meetings and exhorted the listeners to totally give their lives to Jesus. The presence of God increased and many began to find Jesus in life-changing ways. On Sunday, November 6, Roberts and the congregation at Moriah Chapel prayed for a great outpouring of the Holy Spirit, who descended in power that very night as many prayed until early morning the next day. The electric power and presence of God permeated the ensuing revival meetings. Spontaneous prayer and worship, public confession of sin, and powerful testimonies characterized the Holy Spirit–led gatherings. A firsthand witness stated:

> Some people would be crying for joy; others crying for sorrow over
> their sin. Several people would be praying at the same time; for their

friends, parents or children. Some would be singing; others telling people about the joy they now experienced. The chapels were filled to capacity and there were crowds of people on the roads outside. Yet there was no disorder in the meetings. They lasted until 2, 3, or 4 o'clock in the morning so that men coming off the night shift in the colliery met the people coming out of the meetings.[3]

The revival meetings did not depend upon Evan Roberts's presence. In response to the prayers of many others, the Holy Spirit began to move all over Wales in places Roberts never visited. In 1904 and 1905 out of a population of about one million Welsh people, more than one hundred thousand were saved and transformed by the power of God.

The revival drastically changed Welsh society. Policeman lost their jobs as the crime level dropped to extraordinary levels. Dance halls and bars shut down from the lack of customers, and soccer matches were canceled from lack of interest. Magistrates appeared in court but had no cases to try. People began to forgive one another and repay their debts. Many who once used their money for drunkenness began to take care of their families and contribute to the work of God. Even poor confused ponies no longer understood the commands of the miners who previously used curse-laden language to direct them. That is what an awakening looks like!

THE FIRE SPREADS

The great outpouring in Wales eventually spread to all five continents of the world. By 1906 in Los Angeles, California, the fire of the Holy Spirit burned brightly in a former livery stable at 312 Azusa Street. Rumblings of the Spirit had already begun in several other places, but the revival fires burned the brightest in that chapel on Azusa Street. The meetings were led by William Seymour, son of a former slave from Louisiana:

> Thousands came together in worship and prayer; men, women, children, the aged, blacks, whites, Hispanic, Asians, the rich and the poor, the educated and the uneducated all flocked to Los Angeles to attend the Azusa Street Mission Revival. William Seymour held three services a day, seven days a week, for three years. Seymour would tell his believers to talk about Jesus Christ, rather than about talking in tongues.
>
> Seymour led the worship with the help of blacks, whites, men, women, young, and old volunteers. The Revival continued for three years. He continued to serve as the pastor of the Apostolic Faith Mission on Azusa Street along with his wife Jennie Evans Moore, whom he married In May 13, 1908. They lived on top of the mission and organized schools, rescue missions and other congregations, all the time preaching the Holy Ghost baptism and preaching against racism.[4]

1947 REVIVAL IN NORTH AMERICA

In 1947, a significant revival began in America and Canada that became known as both the Healing Revival and the Latter Rain Revival. Many trace the beginning of this post-World War II season of spiritual increase to a meeting in Vancouver, BC, led by a humble, simple preacher named William Branham, a former Baptist who had an unusual word of knowledge and healing ministry.

Signs, wonders, healings, and miracles characterized this outpouring. God used Branham's remarkable word of knowledge gift to release faith and healing in an incredible way. His ministry and that of Oral Roberts encouraged many other ministers who began to have effective healing ministries too.

By 1948, the Healing Revival spread, and a parallel stream known as the Latter Rain Revival began in a meeting of students at Sharon Orphanage and Schools in North Battleford, Saskatchewan, Canada. Inspired by the Branham meetings, three Pentecostal pastors, George Hawtin, P. G. Hunt, and Herrick Holt convened a gathering of students that marked the emergence of a new revival among Pentecostals. By July 1948, thousands gathered at the Sharon Camp Meeting where God healed many and demonstrated His power as people "fell under the power."

The Latter Rain stream contained different emphases from the Healing Revival, although supernatural healings and signs were part of it. Leaders were convinced that Christianity had eroded over the ages and that a return to fundamental apostolic faith was necessary. They emphasized restoration of the five-fold ministry listed in Ephesians 4:11, the unity of the body of Christ, the laying on of hands for the impartation of spiritual gifts, personal prophecy, and the recovery of true worship typified by their understanding of David's tabernacle in the Old Testament.

Much good came out of both these revival streams. But because God uses fallible men and women to carry out His divine plans, there are no perfect or pure revivals. The Latter Rain and the Healing Revival created controversy, and it is true that nonbiblical excesses were found in both movements. But the outpouring was an authentic and fruitful manifestation of the Spirit of God. Many people received healing, and the cry for the restoration of apostles and prophets to the church was greatly needed, as Paul said,

> He Himself gave some to be apostles, some prophets, some evange-
> lists, and some pastors and teachers, for the equipping of the saints
> for the work of ministry, for the edifying of the body of Christ, till

we all come to the unity of the faith and of the knowledge of the Son of God, to a perfect man, to the measure of the stature of the fullness of Christ. (Eph. 4:11–13)

1951 Argentine Revival

In June 1951, the year stamped on my second wheat penny, a move of God began in City Bell, a small town outside of Buenos Aires, Argentina. At a small Bible institute, an angel visited a young student named Alex, who ardently sought more from the Lord. In the history of revivals unusual angelic participation is common.

Alex was praying in a dark field in the starlit early morning hours when an angel approached him in an ever-increasing light. The angel's appearance engulfed the young man in a powerful presence of the Lord, overcoming him with a manifestation of God's love and an overwhelming sense of the fear of the Lord. The boy fled from the angel in terror, running to the Bible school dormitory, only to find the doors locked. He banged on the doors until someone let him in, thinking he would escape the awesome sense of the fear of the Lord. But the angel followed him into the dormitory, and all the students awoke simultaneously from the overwhelming presence.

The fear of the Lord was so strong that the students instantly began to repent of their sins. The next morning, a time of prayer replaced regularly scheduled classes. In great expectation, the students met in a hushed and tearful silence as they waited on the Lord. Then the angelic presence stood beside young Alex.

In a spiritual encounter the angel took Alex to many cities around the world. This young man from the jungles of the Chaco region had only a primary school education and did not know of the many, many cities and nations that the angel showed him. For eight hours, he named place after place in the language of the nation in which he traveled. The angel promised him that the Lord would visit each of these places before His return.

Other times when the angel came, he gave prophetic messages that the students recorded. The prayer meeting continued for four months, characterized by deep repentance and much weeping. The students of the Bible institute continuously prayed for the Lord to be merciful to their nation, pleading for forgiveness of their national sins. As one student prayed, he wept for hours leaning up against a plaster wall. When he finished, often six or eight hours later, his tears formed a puddle in the floor after running down the wall. This encounter continued day after day.

By September, the sorrow turned to laughter, and the group understood that their prayers had been answered. Prophecies about God's filling large venues came. Through a series of remarkable events, Tommy Hicks, an American evangelist fueled with a God-given vision for Argentina, met with Juan Peron, the Argentine president. After Hicks prayed for him, God healed Peron of a serious skin condition. The president gave Hicks access to radio and the press as well as the largest stadium in the nation. By 1954, approximately 25,000 and then 180,000 people attended single gospel meetings. The numerical growth of the church in Argentina exploded.

BACK TO THE FUTURE

What will our future look like? Like Wales in 1904, the United States and Canada in 1947, and Argentina in 1951, with repentance and salvation making a huge impact, with signs and wonders and widespread healing being poured out, with many angelic visitations and multiplied thousands gathering in huge arenas to hear the gospel! What is coming to our nation will contain the fullness of all three of these great outpourings. What was detailed in these historic and documented outpourings was only a preview of what lies in our immediate future. This level of experiential salvation is now closer than when we first believed! We are going "back to the future." Change is at hand.

Seventeen

ANOINTED TO SERVE

A powerful level of anointing is coming, perhaps unlike anything our generation has seen. The ministry of Jesus revealed that the purpose of the anointing is to serve people, to heal all who are oppressed by the devil: "God anointed Jesus of Nazareth with the Holy Spirit and with power, who went about doing good and healing all who were oppressed by the devil, for God was with Him" (Acts 10:38). With great anointing comes public recognition and the temptation to revel in success that is only a product of His grace.

In the past many have fallen prey to spiritual pride, which restricts the favor of God from continuing to flow in our lives. In times of outpouring some have mishandled the anointing and used it for selfish desires. Men and women have fallen, embarrassed themselves, short-circuited the work of God, and caused many to stumble in their faith. May God help us to walk faithfully in the fullness of what He wants to release to our generation.

In a dream the Lord gave me insight into the characteristics and purpose for this anointing. In it I found myself in an expensive clothing store filled with the most marvelous garments. Rack after rack of

177

amazing colorful coats filled the fine establishment. I thought, who wouldn't want one of these extraordinary garments?

As I gazed over the racks of coats, one caught my attention. I carefully pulled it from the racks and tried it on. The coat had a Carolina sky–blue front, a colorful wide-striped back, and a delicate expensive amber leather collar. I looked at myself in a full-length mirror, admiring the fit. The waist-length jacket had unusual three-quarter-length sleeves. It fit me perfectly, as if it had been tailor-made just for me.

Artificial light can affect the appearance of a garment, so I stepped outside to see how it looked in natural light. I was delighted with such a colorful and fine-fitting coat. I turned to go back into the store to pay for it, only to discover that the store was nowhere to be found. It had disappeared—but the coat remained, and it was mine! I could not pay for it.

God will clothe many with tailored coats of favor reminiscent of the coat of many colors Jacob gave his son Joseph. This anointing will release prophetic revelation represented by the coat's heavenly sky-blue garment front.

In the dream I could not pay for the coat. Like salvation, it is free to us, but it came at such a high price that only the Lord Himself could pay for it. The Lord's garments are tailor made for those He chooses to wear them. We must appreciate what a privilege this is and wear and use our garments with humility and wisdom. This new anointing is free, but it will surely cost us something to wear it. It may cost us friends, time, convenience, and popularity, but no one can earn the precious anointing of God.

The stripes on the back of the coat speak of a healing anointing provided by the Lord Jesus as a result of the stripes He suffered during

His scourging. The prophet Isaiah foresaw that the sufferings of Jesus produced the potential for divine healing when he prophesied, "He was wounded for our transgressions, He was bruised for our iniquities; the chastisement for our peace was upon Him, and by His stripes we are healed" (Isa. 53:5).

PROPHETIC EVIDENCE

God often uses natural events as prophetic pictures to reveal spiritual truth. On December 15, 2014, a magnitude 3.0 earthquake occurred in Caldwell County near Newland, North Carolina, at approximately 1:44 a.m. Many people reported that the earthquake sounded like an explosion violently shaking houses. One woman thought a car had hit her house because it shook so much. She got out of bed and went outside expecting to find the car that hit her house. She did not find one.

Newland, the county seat of Caldwell County, is the highest (literal altitude) seat of government on the Eastern Seaboard. This location signifies a new "high level of authority" over sickness. That authority will be so profound that people will be healed by authoritative proclamation, simply by being "called well."

TAILOR-MADE HEALING

Years ago a friend and I prayed for a woman named Lori Taylor who had cancer. Her kind of cancer had already claimed the lives of two of her close relatives. As we prayed for her, and with no thought about her last name, by faith I reached into the kingdom of heaven and proclaimed a *"tailor-made"* healing for our friend. As I made the proclamation I noticed Taylor Caldwell's book *Great Lion of God* on the shelf immediately behind her. I suddenly realized I just asked for a *tailor*-made healing for a woman named Lori *Taylor*. As the book title and the author's name registered with me, I called well Lori Taylor in the name of Christ Jesus, the Great Lion of God. Lori went on to take treatment for her cancer, and God completely healed her. In essence she received a "Taylor called-well" healing from the Great Lion of God. A new level of healing anointing is coming.

THE COLLAR

The expensive amber-colored leather collar of my dream reveals that everything of high spiritual value must be paid for with shed blood. Just as the Lord shed the blood of animals to cover Adam and Eve with leather garments after the fall, so this garment has been sanctified by the blood of the Son of God.

The amber-colored collar also speaks of both the glory of God and the harvest. In Ezekiel 1, the prophet saw that amber was the color of the glory of God. In our song "America the Beautiful," one of the lines describes the harvest as "amber waves of grain." So the garment I saw is for serving the purpose of the coming great harvest and the manifest glory of God that will accompany it.

JOSEPH'S COAT

Joseph's colorful coat provides more insight into characteristics of this anointing: "Now Israel loved Joseph more than all his children, because he was the son of his old age. Also he made him a tunic of many colors" (Gen. 37:3).

Jacob gave Joseph the coat because of his great love for his son. God is giving us these coats because of His great love for the world that needs His healing. The many colors in Joseph's coat spoke of the favor of God that manifests as the manifold wisdom of God and the prophetic wisdom that enabled Joseph to preserve the future nation of

Israel in a time of great famine. God will once again grant the kind of wisdom that can save entire nations.

Joseph's coat was one of great promise, giftedness, and authority. It represented the favor of Joseph's father, Jacob, and pointed to Joseph as the future primary leader of his family.

FREE BUT EXPENSIVE

In my dream I could not pay for the coat. It was a gift to me, paid for by someone else. But as many have discovered, some free gifts are expensive to own. Walking in this great anointing will be costly too. In Joseph's case the coat was the focus of his brothers' jealousy and hatred. This new coat may generate similar responses from those who don't understand why God anoints those He does. Ultimately his brothers stripped Joseph of his coat, sold him into slavery, dipped the coat in blood, and lied to their father about wild animals killing him. They stole his coat, but they could not destroy God's favor or the powerful spiritual gifts He gave him.

It was necessary for Joseph to lose the outward sign of the anointing and be tested in order to function at the highest level the robe initially promised. The jealousy and hatred of his brothers were part of the price Joseph paid to live out the gift he was given. The blood-soaked garment revealed that every anointing must be sanctified for it to be ultimately successful.

When Moses anointed Aaron and his sons for service, he stripped them, washed them, clothed them, and *then* anointed them. Afterward he sanctified them with blood: "He took some of its blood and put it on the tip of Aaron's right ear, on the thumb of his right hand, and on the big toe of his right foot. Then he brought Aaron's sons. And Moses put some of the blood on the tips of their right ears, on the thumbs of their right hands, and on the big toes of their right feet" (Lev. 8:23–24).

How many men and women have forfeited their anointing because they did not submit to the entire process meant to ensure the success of the ministry gifts God gave them? We must embrace this process of the Lord if we are to *wear* His anointing successfully. Many allow jealousy and selfish ambition to short-circuit this process. Such attitudes and actions release much evil and thwart our ability to function effectively. Scripture says, "If you have bitter envy and self-seeking in your hearts, do not boast and lie against the truth. This wisdom does not descend from above, but is earthly, sensual, demonic. For where envy and self-seeking exist, confusion and every evil thing are there" (James 3:14–16).

THREE-QUARTER-LENGTH SLEEVES

Shortly after having the dream, my wife and I ate at an old-school southern drive-in restaurant. We ordered our food through the carside intercom, and a server brought it out. His uniform caught my eye, as he wore a red servant's coat with three-quarter-length sleeves, just like the coat's sleeves in my dream. The colorful coat is for serving others. Too often, anointed people misuse God's gifts to serve only themselves. This coat must not be used that way.

God freely gives colorful mantles, but with each one comes a price. Joseph graduated from God's school of the anointing and ruled in Egypt with wisdom, dignity, mercy, and kindness. His understanding of God's redemptive ways and his victory over self-centeredness and bitterness enabled him to revive his father's household and preserve the lineage of the Messiah. The true purpose of the anointing is not to make our own ministry successful, although it may. Its primary function is to serve others and fulfill the Lord's purpose.

Joseph used his anointing to empower and enrich many who had lost their inheritance. This new anointing also has the potential to restore households, free prisoners, reclaim legacies, and declare the glory of God through the lives of redeemed people.

Prepare your hearts, for this cherished and challenging anointing is available even now. Wear your new royal garment with wisdom, humility, and dignity. Joseph's anointing served to revive his father's household. God is poised to clothe us with an anointing that will again revive His household.

THE GARMENT OF HOPE

Joseph's coat of many colors was a garment of hope. It speaks of being the Father's favorite and clothed with His great love, a truth that echoes God's heart for each of His children. The coat's many beautiful colors point to the variety of beautiful blessings and spiritual gifts God has for us that enable us to excel and thrive in this life and empower us to serve those around us. Its many colors also remind us of the beauty of the rainbow, an ancient symbol of our covenant-keeping God's promise to never again destroy mankind with rain and floods.

To Joseph that coat was a garment of hope, a symbol of the promise he had for a successful future. That hope enabled him to endure hardship, betrayal, slander, and imprisonment to emerge as one equipped to save the ancient world, his own dysfunctional family, and the lineage of the Messiah Himself.

The world is searching for a sustainable life of hope. Over the last eight years, the Bible app YouVersion has been downloaded more than three hundred million times. Two of the most downloaded verses come from the prophets Joshua and Jeremiah:

Be strong and of good courage; do not be afraid, nor be dismayed, for the LORD your God is with you wherever you go. (Josh. 1:9)

I know the thoughts that I think toward you, says the LORD, thoughts of peace and not of evil, to give you a future and a hope. (Jer. 29:11)

Many have looked for that hope in worldly things that seemed to offer it, but they could not deliver. That search ends when any hungry soul finds the reality of the gospel of the kingdom of God and the man Christ Jesus the Lord, our true Harbinger of Hope.

NOTES

CHAPTER 2: THE FIVE WAGONS
1. Roswell D. Hitchcock, *Hitchcock's Bible Names Dictionary* (S.i.: Benediction Classics, Oxford, 2010).

CHAPTER 9: PRISONERS OF HOPE
1. Ronald F. Youngblood, *Nelson's Illustrated Bible Dictionary* (Nashville, TN: HarperCollins Christian Pub., 2014).

CHAPTER 11: HOPE RESTORED
1. Ronald F. Youngblood, *Nelson's Illustrated Bible Dictionary* (Nashville, TN: HarperCollins Christian Pub., 2014).
2. Peter Robinson, *How Ronald Reagan Changed My Life* (New York: HarperCollins e-Books, 2014).

CHAPTER 12: ACCESSING THE BLESSINGS OF HEAVEN
1. "Ichiro visits Sisler's grave," ESPN.com, July 15, 2009, www.espn.com/mlb/news/story?id=4329684.
2. Ibid.

CHAPTER 13: THE POWER OF THE HOLY SPIRIT
1. Fr. Raniero Cantalamessa is a leader in the Catholic Charismatic renewal. https://shop.franciscanmedia.org/products/sober-intoxication-of-the-spirit-filled-with-the-fullness-of-god.

2. Fr. James Martin on the Humor of St. Teresa of Ávila/News/Order of Carmelites. From Carmelites.net.

3. Ibid.

4. James Martin, SJ, *America: The Jesuit Review*, April 2, 2007.

5. Word #3196 from *Strong's Concordance*, www.blueletterbible.org/lang /lexicon/lexicon.cfm?strongs=H3196.

6. David Brown, Matthew-John, vol. 5, in *A Commentary; Critical, Experimental and Practical, on the Old and New Testaments*, edited by Robert Jamieson, A. R. Fausset, David Brown (Grand Rapids, MI: Eerdmans, 1946).

Chapter 15: The Power of Forgiveness

1. Jim Hill, *Impenetrable: Breaking the Curse of Racial Hatred* (CreateSpace Independent Publishing Platform, 2017). Used by permission.

Chapter 16: The Coming Harvest

1. "ANZAC Prophetic List," Monday, July 14, 2003, "It Happened 200 Years Ago: The Great Revival," by Jim Brooks.

2. Excerpts from the Emancipation Proclamation, abrahamlincolnonline.org, Speeches and Writings, Emancipation Proclamation.

3. "1904 Revival," *Moriah Chapel*, accessed March 11, 2018, http://www .moriahchapel.org.uk/index.php?page=1904-revival.

4. Joanne Holstein, "Azusa (Asusa) Street Revival, Birth of the Pentecostal Movement," April 27, 2015, Guided Bible Studies, Guidedbiblestudies.com.

About the Author

Robin McMillan is the founder and senior pastor of Queen City Church in Charlotte, North Carolina. He believes that the next Great Awakening of the American church is imminent. His passion is to awaken her to the power of the Holy Spirit and enable believers to discover how to access the realm of the heavens and enjoy the presence and power of God. With a unique preaching style, prophetic giftings, and a desire for the release of God's presence, outpourings of the Holy Spirit and demonstrations of power often accompany his ministry. Robin and his wife, Donna, have four children and five grandchildren. He currently resides in Fort Mill, South Carolina.

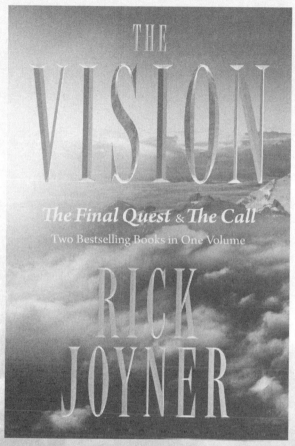